CHINESE MONUMENTAL ART

CHINESE MONUMENTAL ART

PETER C. SWANN

Photographs by Claude Arthaud and
François Hébert-Stevens

157 plates, 14 in colour
15 maps and diagrams

THAMES AND HUDSON · LONDON

To Professors S. Mizuno and T. Nagahiro of Kyoto, Japan,
to whose labours we are all indebted

THE PHOTOGRAPHERS would like to express their gratitude to the authorities of the People's Republic of China who allowed them to visit and photograph monuments scattered over the whole expanse of China.
They also wish to thank the Musée Guimet, the Musée Cernuschi and the Freer Gallery, Washington, D.C., for the very kind way in which they allowed them access to the most rare pieces in their collections.

AUTHOR'S NOTE: This book is the outcome of a visit which two brilliant photographers, François Hébert-Stevens and Claude Arthaud, recently paid to China. They brought back many valuable photographic documents worthy of a permanent record. My text attempts to link them into an intelligible whole. Needless to say, their selection was in no way complete; to have made it so would have meant very extensive additions which would have detracted from the unity and *in situ* quality of their record. In some minor instances it proved impossible to identify the actual site of the photographed subject. Many of them are here reproduced for the first time and should enlarge our knowledge of Chinese sculpture.

CONTENTS

LIST OF MAPS AND FIGURES

LIST OF PLATES

INTRODUCTION: BUDDHISM

A GREAT MANY of the finest examples of monumental art in China owe their creation to Buddhist inspiration. For this reason it might be helpful by way of introduction to examine the way in which Buddhism was adapted by the Chinese and into what cultural tradition, as well as very briefly to describe the nature of Buddhism itself.

The monuments of China reproduced in this book span a period of two thousand years. They are the products of one of the world's most individual cultures. In the history of civilization such independent cultural systems are comparatively few; they include the ancient Near East, Egypt, pre-Columbian South America, Europe, India and China. Of them all, the Chinese shares with the Indian the longest unbroken tradition. Of the two, that of China has on the whole been least influenced by other cultures. The material remains of China's past give evidence of prodigious vitality, resilience and refinement. Whatever it created has the unmistakable imprint of its genius.

Chinese civilization grew up in isolation and accepted little from beyond its natural boundaries, except for the one major impact which came from India. A large part of this book is concerned with Indian influence on Chinese art, of artistic, religious and philosophical ideas from a land which had developed a fundamentally different way of life and thought, because it was from India that Buddhism came to China. In this respect China was for a time a country invaded by religious missionaries, but the Chinese solved the problems created by the arrival of Indian culture with Buddhism in their own particular manner!

However, the influence on China of Indian Buddhism and all the traditions to which it was heir is only part of a long history—in fact it occupies at most only one thousand of about four thousand years of unbroken civilization in this centre of the Far East. In order to understand Chinese non-Buddhist art as well as their remarkable Buddhist monuments, it is important to consider briefly some of the fundamentals of Chinese artistic thought, to map out some of the underlying aspects and principal lines. Unless we appreciate the foundation of native culture it is impossible to understand what China made of this great invasion.

The country is very large. China proper, which includes the valleys of the great rivers, the Yellow River, the Yangtze and the Hsi Kiang, is about two-fifths of the size of Europe. Apart from the eighteen provinces of this central area there are another ten or more which comprise the areas known as Tibet, Sinkiang, Manchuria and Mongolia. Thus, the present-day area of China is somewhat greater than the whole of Europe. China proper, a land of about a million and a half square miles, is defined by natural boundaries which from earliest times isolated it—the sea on the east, the cold lands of the steppes to the north, the deserts and mountains of Central Asia and Tibet to the west and the forbidding jungles to the south. Its most vulnerable frontier has always been that in the north and the various nomad peoples who have arisen in these cold northern lands have played a very considerable role both in Chinese history and in the history of India and the West. Chinese policy has for millennia been dictated by the dire necessity of excluding these fierce and destructive peoples from the rich, settled homelands of China. At the same time the nomads have contributed in one way or another much more to Chinese culture than most historians, certainly Chinese historians, have credited them with. They have been the only conquerors of China. They governed all or part of China proper for about seven hundred years, and their ways of life and their art left a permanent mark on those of China. They first brought the eastern and the western worlds together, and above all, they were the first great sponsors of Buddhism. Under them Buddhism became for the first time a national religion.

When the Great Wall was first built in the 3rd century BC, Chinese civilization was already nearly fifteen hundred years old. These formative centuries which constitute the Chinese bronze age were, towards the end, marked by intense inter-state warfare and equally intense intellectual speculation. During this period a consciousness of unity of culture already found expression in art. However, no idea of political unity existed. These were the centuries of Chinese history during which the country emerged from a stone age to an advanced bronze age whose products far outshine those of all other civilizations at a similar stage in their development. The last capital of the Shang dynasty (c. 1500–1027 BC) at An-yang (c. 1300–1027 BC) has yielded bronze vessels of unsurpassed technique and grandeur—reflections of which can be seen in many subsequent periods of Chinese art. One can find a porcelain vase of the 18th century whose shape is inspired by a bronze of 1000 BC. These bronzes show, in addition to their extraordinarily fine technique, a boldness of line, an acute appreciation of form and above all a gift for imparting a sense of monumentality to even the smallest object. This bronze art persisted, with diminishing power, down to the time of the Han dynasty (206 BC–AD 220).

The period from the 6th to the 1st centuries BC saw the flowering of native Chinese thought. During this period the so-called 'Hundred Schools' of philosophy flourished. Many of these 'schools' left no trace after the First Emperor, at the end of the 3rd century BC, in an attempt to wipe out the memories of any ways of thought other than his own, and in a manner typical of many dictators, burnt their books and ruthlessly suppressed their followers. However, at least three of these schools have left a deep impression on China—Confucianism, Taoism and Legalism.

Confucianism is essentially the moralists' way. Confucius was an idealist who preached a return to an ideal and largely illusory past. A failed politician, he had the misfortune to live in a period of political anarchy, of power politics. According to his theory, a perfect emperor ruled a people who automatically modelled themselves on his perfection. The men who governed should be cultured gentlemen, highly conservative in outlook, benign in action, and accordingly the society they governed would automatically be contented and obedient. Loyalty, culture and education were the touchstones, the pervading principles, the civilizing influences.

Taoism appealed to the other side of human nature, to the mystical, illogical inactive side of the human spirit. It encouraged man to seek union with supra-human powers, with the Tao or 'the Way', the First Principle of the Universe which pervades all things and which can enrich immeasurably the being who achieves the desired union. The means to this union was through non-action, not a negative but a positive non-action through which all things are accomplished. Part of this theory involved the preservation of the vital energy in all beings. What started as a profound mysticism ended as a method of popular magic seeking recipes for immortality through alchemy, long life through breath control, preservation and increase in one's vital powers through the interruption of the sexual act, etc. This creed, more irrational and perhaps more immediately rewarding than the duller tenets of Confucian morality, prepared the Chinese spirit for the infinitely richer mysticism of Buddhist thought.

The third early Chinese way of thought was Legalism—the rule of law, the amoral theory according to which mankind was essentially evil and must be coerced. This theory created the state of Ch'in, the most powerful state among the many of the Warring States period (460–221 BC) and, through Ch'in's triumph, led to the unification of China.

All three theories have left their mark on Chinese thought and art.

The moral outlook of Confucianism with its emphasis on the complete cultured man encouraged an interest in the arts and an appreciation of their value to society. It encouraged conservatism and formalism, it stressed the value of study and knowledge. Although it stated a preference for conservatism, the value of transmitting without creating, it did not decry the importance of innovation. It placed learning above all things, and this is no mean contribution to the culture of a people. Confucius preserved China's past and laid down the principles which guided the education of the governing class of China for nearly two thousand years. His creed gave China a fundamental appreciation of humane conduct and, as interpreted by followers like Mencius, it made the Chinese familiar with the concept of compassion— a basic tenet of Buddhism.

Taoism was equally important in that it taught man to look beyond the externals of life into the deeper phenomena of existence, to seek the secrets of life, to identify himself with the creative energy of nature. It taught humility, passivity, receptivity. Legalism had perhaps the least immediate effect on the arts, but it unified and disciplined China and gave it a conviction of the inevitability of this unity. It expressed the practicality and realism inherent in the Chinese mentality which, from being applied first to politics, then pervaded all aspects of Chinese life. It condemned tradition and extolled ends rather than means. It decried book learning and the arts, magic and ritual as unprofitable. It taught the value of discipline, and its harshness produced a violent reaction towards Confucianism in the Han dynasty. It produced in China the strange phenomenon of one humane cultured law for the intellectual and another harsher code for the simple. When the battle between the Buddhist Church and the State became critical in the 9th century AD, it was the state, founded on Legalist principles, which won.

All three in their individual ways contributed to the success of Buddhism. From a negative point of view Confucianism had excluded metaphysics and distrusted the gods. It offered a relatively unattractive after-life, in which the dead for a few generations received respectful sacrifices in the role of ancestors. On the positive side it taught men the value of a moral life centred around a just emperor and his upright ministers. This the Buddhist teachers easily interpreted as the Buddha and his heavenly hosts. Confucius stressed the importance of the renewal of the self, the Buddhist aimed at the renewal of life. According to the latter, the Confucian perfection of the man held little and arid prospects, whereas the Buddhist perfection of the spirit led to infinite blessings. Confucianism taught man to be content with his lot, Buddhism promised greater rewards for the same virtue. The Confucian quality of obedience was equally important to the Buddhist. The Confucians emphasized the importance of the study of ancient literature and this reverence for texts served the Buddhists when the vast literature of their faith came to China. The Confucians stressed the value of a proper observance of the rites which also formed an important part of Buddhist teaching. Even the cult of the ancestors found an immediate reflection in the cult of the historical Buddha and the many divinities of the Greater Vehicle.

Taoism familiarized China with metaphysics and mysticism which take a large place in Buddhist thought. The theories of reality, the absolute, underlying principles of all life, available only through mystical experiencies, were easily adopted and adapted to serve Buddhist aims. Taoism, like Buddhism, contained an anti-social element. As the Confucians complained, priests and monks contributed nothing to the material wealth of the country. Familiarity with Taoist priests made the arrival of the large numbers of Buddhist priests and missionaries seem quite normal. In fact Buddhism at first masqueraded as a form of Taoism.

Legalism gave the man in the street a healthy respect for the law and it was easy to transfer this respect to the Buddhist law. It taught discipline, and without discipline a monastic order and meditation, both fundamentals of Buddhism, are impossible. It extolled the power of the king and this proved useful to the Buddhist Church. As well as its harsh penalties for transgression, it offered rewards for good behaviour. This idea, transferred to a religious sphere, is essentially Buddhism at its most popular level.

Buddhism reached China at a critical moment in Chinese history. The greatest moment of the Han dynasty was passed and Confucian standards had completely broken down. Confucianism had shown itself incapable of preventing disaster. At the same time, China's vision had expanded beyond the limits of the country itself. Military adventures in Central Asia had made men realize that China was not the whole world, not perhaps even the centre of the world, and it had stimulated intellectual curiosity regarding other peoples and their cultures. At the same time the collapse of the Han dynasty and the political decay which followed it left a vacuum which none of the existing doctrines seemed able to fill. Buddhism appeared as a religion of salvation.

Knowledge of Buddhism has spread greatly throughout the West, but it might be useful to give some idea of the religion which was to conquer China. Like all religious art, Buddhist art cannot be understood without some knowledge of the religion and its founder. As with the life of Christ, that of the Buddha is full of events which have inspired centuries of artists both in his home country and across the vast areas of the Far East into which Buddhism penetrated. It should be remembered that, in its finest hour, Buddhism had more adherents than any of the world's religions has ever claimed. Its art, from India through China to Japan, is one of the great glories of man.

Like Christ, the Buddha was a historical figure, but born nearly six centuries before Him. His father, Suddhodana, was a wealthy chief of a small Āryan tribe called the Sākyas in the City of Kapilavastu, North India. His family name was Gautama, but the son is usually known by the name, Sākyamuni. Tradition tells of his great physical beauty and high intelligence. In spite of the advantages of birth and wealth, being surrounded with every form of luxury, his spirit was, nevertheless, troubled and deep inner happiness seemed to elude him. Even a beautiful wife and son failed to bring him contentment. On three occasions when he happened to ride out of his castle, he met three of the principal reasons for sorrow—old age, sickness and death—in the form of human beings. These were said to have been sent by the gods to remind him of the sadder aspects of this life. He determined to discover why living beings suffered and thence how to escape the pain on which the world seemed to be built. During his meditation on these problems, on the fourth occasion when he left his castle, he met a homeless ascetic. The calm features of this man showed that here at least was someone seeking to solve the problem of the pain inherent in the transience of all things. Determined that he, too, would seek in similar solitude deliverance for himself and all mankind, he slipped away from his castle in the middle of the night. The stories of what is called the 'Great Renunciation' and the events leading up to it are often depicted in Buddhist art. His wife is seen sleeping with her maids around her while the Prince leaves the palace. The life of pleasure is depicted, and the sculptors try to express the inner struggle which his renunciation caused him. His birth in the Lumbini Park is a popular representation, for he was said to have been delivered from his mother's side while she supported herself by holding a branch of a tree. One of the most frequent representations is the scene of his Departure from the Palace in which heavenly beings are shown supporting his horse's hooves in order that no sound should reach the sleeping household. He is sometimes shown in the forest bidding farewell to his white horse which kneels before him. His victories over the forces of evil, his moment of enlightenment and, of course, his death, provide many other scenes.

The Prince then started on the second great period of his life in which he sought

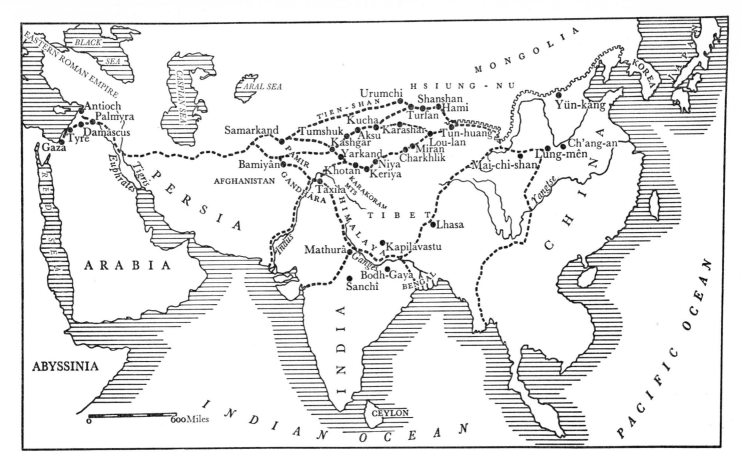

1 *Routes across Central Asia (c. AD 300–600). Note the Silk Route joining Mediterranean markets to Asia. From Tun-huang pilgrims for India either went north via Kucha or south via Khotan.*

truth in the traditional Indian way as a homeless ascetic. The stories of his temptations in the wilderness have something in common with those of Christ. After some years of study he decided that the solution to his problems was not to be found in the Brahmanical teachings, which emphasized the need for man to spiritualize his inner self. This, he felt, was only a balm and not a radical cure of man's sorrows. Man was still bound by a chain of birth and rebirth from which he could not escape.

He then decided to win salvation through the traditional method of austerities, hoping thereby to free his soul from his body. Reducing his food to almost nothing, the Prince wasted away almost to the point of death. But this method, too, failed him and he took food to regain his strength before entering into his last trial—that of the most profound meditation. Under the Bodhi tree he sat during one more night of the most testing temptations at the end of which, as dawn broke, he achieved enlightenment, saw the innermost secrets of birth, death and rebirth and the final way of escape. At this moment, he became the Buddha, 'The Enlightened One'.

15

The third period of his life was spent in spreading his teaching throughout the north-east of India.

He preached the impermanence of the life of the senses and the way of salvation through purity of thought, word and deed. According to him there were Four Truths through which the pain of birth and rebirth could be stopped; these involve an appreciation of ill, what it is, what it comes from, and of the Eightfold Path by which it can be stopped. The Eightfold Path consists of Right Views, Right Intentions, Right Speech, Right Conduct, Right Livelihood, Right Effort, Right Meditation, and Right Mindfulness.

His following grew rapidly, miracles as astounding as those of Christ are recounted and he was recognized everywhere as the founder of a new sect within the old Hindu tradition.

At the age of eighty his end grew near. His death or *pari-nirvāṇa*, 'the complete extinction of self-hood as well as the material on which it is built', is as frequently represented in Buddhist art as is the crucifixion of Christ. With his sorrowing disciples around him he entered into his final ecstasy and passed into this *pari-nirvāṇa*—the final release. His body was burned and the relics divided—their fate over the centuries was as chequered as that of the fragments of the true cross of Christ. In 1956 the 2,500th anniversary of this event was celebrated throughout the world.

After the death of the Buddha, his teachings spread still further. Certain of them have had the most far-reaching importance in the history of Asia. Their subsequent development as a religion, especially in the forms accepted in China and Japan, deeply influenced the arts of these countries. Buddhism flourished in India for over fifteen hundred years till the coming of Islam (10th–12th centuries) and it survives to this day in Ceylon, Burma, Siam, Tibet and Nepal. It spread like fire through Central Asia and to China and Japan where it set alight the imaginations of peoples ripe for a spiritual awakening.

The Buddha's doctrine evolved in various schools, which, about five hundred years after his death, formed two main divisions, the *hinayāna* (or Lesser Vehicle) and the *mahāyāna* (or Greater Vehicle). In *hinayāna*, although the laity also shared in the benefits of Buddhism, the tendency was to stress the life of the secluded monk as the way to salvation. The great difference between this and the *mahāyāna* was the

1   BUDDHA, surrounded by his disciples—figures of painted clay. Cave CCV, Tun-huang, Kansu province (6th–7th century).

elaboration in the latter of the concept of *bodhisattvas*. These were mortals who, through merit, gained in past lives, were entitled to become Buddhas but, through compassion for suffering humanity, delayed the final consummation. Thus the *mahāyāna* greatly increased the numerous assembly of heavenly and ghostly beings developed by the *hinayāna*. It was mainly the *mahāyāna* form which reached China and Japan and the bodhisattva concept which appealed to their peoples.*

P. C. Swann: *An Introduction to the Arts of Japan*. Oxford, 1958. Any reader who wishes to know more about this profound religion should read Edward Conze, *Buddhism*. Oxford, 1951.

After the intensity and anguish of two centuries of warfare following the fall of the Han dynasty in AD 221, Buddhism came not only as a new religion, but also as one which offered a practical solution to the political problem of ending warfare. The Chinese had not known peace for many centuries. The constant wars of the Warring States period had been followed by the costly military expeditions of the Han. The last centuries of this dynasty had been far from peaceful. At the same time the unity and security of the country depended upon settled conditions and made peace an economic necessity.

Apart from the economic need for a way of life which brought peace, Buddhism made a direct appeal to the spirit such as the Chinese had never experienced, even from Taoism. Buddhism promised a blissful life after death equally to the common uneducated man as well as to the educated and select few. Taoism on its metaphysical side had been open to few. Confucianism appealed only to the educated administrator class. Both demanded a highly literate following at a time when literacy was a privilege. Buddhism, however, was available to the humblest, both as simple devotees and also in the fullest sense: the religious way of life in the monasteries was open to all. The monastic life made a great appeal during periods of political uncertainty. Even women could become nuns. Buddhism in fact offered salvation spiritually, politically and economically to all who accepted the vow.

However, the Chinese were highly selective in their faith. The Indian mind is perhaps the most subtle in the world. The Chinese are basically among the most practical and worldly of people. Not for them the ultimate bliss of annihilation in *nirvāna*. Nor do we feel that they appreciated the theory of the pain on which the world is founded and which is inherent in the series of rebirths which precede *nirvāna*. They are not by nature a gloomy or pessimistic people. They seem to have been attracted by the grandeur of Buddhist thought: the infinite panoramas of mul-

2 THE DISCIPLES Ananda and Kāsyapa—figures of painted clay. Cave CCV, Tunhuang, Kansu province (6th–7th century).

tiple Buddha figures, the colourful pageantry, the promise of a paradise in which they could enjoy perfect happiness. The intellectual appreciated the metaphysics, the historical vistas, the close arguments, the wealth of myth and magic, the wide learning, perhaps above all the discipline of meditation whose objective was more worthy than the restricted Chinese aims of popular Taoism. The Lesser Vehicle meant little to the Chinese and never prospered, and from the Greater Vehicle they took what they understood, liked and could use. The closest simile is with the Roman Catholic Church in the West, whose strength lies in that it attracts both the mystic and the intellectual while at the same time providing an impressive pageantry for the simple and a faith in ultimate salvation. There is fundamentally little difference between the approaches of a worshipper who says fifty 'Hail Marys' and one who intones the Buddha's name a thousand times.

To understand how the Chinese were highly selective in their approach to Buddhism, it is important to know a little of the complicated background to Indian history and to the Buddhist religion which it created.

The period of Indian history of particular interest in this respect is from about the 6th century BC to about the end of the 8th century. Already by the time of the birth of the Buddha, India, under the Āryans, the nomadic herdsmen who conquered the North Indian plains, had a religion peopled with numerous gods. These are described in their religious literature, the Vedas, Brāhmaṇas and Upaniṣads (1500–500 BC). Indra, heroic god of war and weather, Sūrya, the sun god, Agni, the fire god, Soma, the king of plants, Varuṇa, the creator and guardian of the cosmic order and punisher of evil, Yama, lord of the dead, Rudra, who brought plague but also could heal, Vāyu, the wind god, and a host of lesser gods and demigods all found in the Rig-Veda, the earliest Indian sacred text. Very early the Indians had developed a sense of what is holy and of sainthood. Sacrifice played an all important part in early Indian religion and this was in the hands of the Brāhmins, a caste whose members only of the whole community possessed supernatural power, the tribal priests and magicians.

The Āryans were a nomadic people and their gods were likewise not localized but general, broad concepts. By the end of the Rig-Vedic period the idea of a creator god arose. Earlier the belief had been current that the world was produced when the gods, his children, sacrificed the Cosmic plan (Prajāpati). Sacrifice, 'the manipulation of the forces of nature in the form of divine personages', in the hands of the Brāhmins became a supernatural mystery and they alone could preserve the regular order of nature. The priests thus became all important. The concept of the transmigration of souls and of *karma,* the results of one life affecting the next, were already elaborated by the 7th and 6th centuries BC.

From the Brāhmin way of life there developed the ascetic's way to knowledge, freedom and magical power. The Upaniṣads, for instance, were 'esoteric philosophical dialogues treating of the realization of the transcendent Self. This philosophical movement, which seems to have become prevalent in the 8th century BC, culminated in the century of the Buddha (*c.* 563–483), who himself was but one of the numerous Indian teachers then pointing the way to spiritual liberation (Mokṣa), absolute illumination (Bodhi) and transcendant repose (Nirvāṇa)'. The ordinary hermit could find in it honour, respect and freedom from care. The higher seeker after knowledge could find in it undefinable insight. 'Gradually plumbing the cosmic mystery, his soul entered realms far beyond the comparatively tawdry heavens where the great gods dwelt in light and splendour. Going "from darkness to darkness deeper yet" he solved the mystery beyond all mysteries; he understood, fully and finally, the nature of the universe and of himself, and he reached a realm of truth and bliss, beyond birth and death, joy and sorrow, good and evil.'* Mysticism is found in most religions, but in India it is a fundamental means.

The desire to find an explanation of the mysteries of creation motivated the minds of the great thinkers of early India. The solutions put forward were many and among them the part played by sexual activity is important in early as in later times both as a means to mystical experience, spiritual intensification, and even as a symbol of divine force. Few civilizations have produced as rich and fertile a period of intellectual speculation as the 6th and 7th centuries BC in India. In this atmosphere of speculation into creation and the nature of self and immortality, the most profound problems which have concerned mankind, the heterodox doctrine of Buddhism was born.

Enquiry into the many profundities of Indian thought in the centuries before and immediately after Buddhism would lead too far, but it is important to appreciate that China had nothing comparable. Indeed it would seem from their literature that the Chinese were little interested in the problems of the origin of creation, in the exploration of the deeper parts of the mind and the self and even in the gods. By comparison they are a truly agnostic people. The climate must have contributed greatly to this difference. China is cold in the winter and its land does not support the ascetic and hermit with the generosity of India. Goetz has defined the factors which formed the Indian character as follows: 'The heat enervates him, sets him dreaming, lets the most improbable events appear possible. But the coolness of the winter and the monsoon awakens a more intense sensitivity and enthusiasm for the

Joseph Campbell in Henrich Zimmer: *The Art of Indian Asia.* New York, 1955, p. 5.

21

beauties of life, and arouses an energy when nothing seems beyond reach. Man is the slave as well as the lord of the universe. Both reactions, however, arouses an intense sexuality, without the inhibitions of our occidental world, frank, but also delicate; and this exuberant sexuality is in its turn restrained by the fear of being completely absorbed by it, by the desire to preserve one's own personality and free will, if necessary at the price of denying sexuality completely.'*

H. Goetz: *India*. London, 1959.

Such a dichotomy and the problems it created never seem to have worried the Chinese. Although they, like most peoples, always had a thorough appreciation of the pleasures of the flesh, their approach to them is comparatively uncomplicated and they play a small part in their early beliefs. Some of their earliest songs dating back to the 8th century BC spring from a background of simple mating and love making. The Taoists looked somewhat deeper and sought the preservation of vital energy through retaining the semen in intercourse and their explanation of the universe was based on a simple duality of procreation through the interplay of male and female, darkness and light, *yin* and *yang* forces. Apart from the *yin* and *yang* theories, the general outlook was comparatively prosaic, and relations between the sexes, especially as laid down by the Confucians, were circumscribed, utilitarian, and, by Indian standards, it must be confessed, somewhat naïve.

One would seek in vain for any suggestion that union with a beautiful woman was the highest bliss to be experienced beyond the full knowledge gained only in the highest states of transcendence. Chinese literature contains a few erotic passages, but the terms used to express intimacy are so symbolic and discreet that they are available only to the scholars and initiated. Chinese poetry has its love poems, but none dwell in detail on the languorous beauty, the physical details of the loved one—her full breasts, wide hips and slim waist, her perfume and her gait. The *mithuna*, couples of lovers in various intimate poses, played no part in Chinese art. China has had its eroticism, but, unlike India, it is neither frank nor fundamental. The Chinese are a practical people more concerned with problems of government than with those of the soul, with ethics rather than with metaphysics, and on the most worldly level with the family rather than with love.

Equally they do not see life in the same pessimistic way as the Indians. The Indians tend to stress the eternal aspects of the universe, the unchanging, the immutable. For the Chinese there is always the prospect of change and of betterment. They are not so weighed down with the results of actions in former lives nor with the prospects of actions in this life affecting future lives. In fact the problems of life after death had appealed to them very little until the arrival of Buddhism. And without this tradition of eternity, the Chinese tended to take a much shorter view of the rewards for a good life. They were far more ready to settle for an immediate paradise, than to delay this consummation for the benefit of greater rewards in a vague transcendental state.

In the same way the Indian vision of the human body and of the female body in particular differs fundamentally from that of the Chinese. The never-ending fascination for the Indian of the female body has produced in art what Zimmer calls an 'everlasting contribution of the Hindu spirit to the treasury of the fair vision of the ages'.

Indian literature abounds in descriptions of the female that are some of the most beautiful and intimate in the world's poetry. Without exploring the wealth of this type of writing in the middle ages and later, it will suffice to quote a few typical lines by the most famous Indian poet, Kālidāsa, writing about AD 400.

> '*While languid maidens, decked with shining gems,*
> *Disclose their beauties, courting the cold air.*'
> '*Clad in light silks voluptuous forms recline,*
> *With breast exhaling sandal wood's perfume.*'
> '*Slender waists set off with golden zones*
> *Breasts all hung with pearls.*'*

Ritusamhara. Trans.: Satyam Jayati. London, 1867.

It would be unthinkable for a Chinese poet to write such verses as:

> '*There she, may be a girl of sylph-like form,*
> *With oval teeth, ripe bimba lips,*
> *Slender waist and deep-set navel,*
> *Her glances as the startled antelope's,*
> *Moving with measured steps*
> *Beneath the burden of her thighs,*
> *And slightly stooping under her twin breasts;*
> *A Creator's pattern of perfect womanhood.*'*

Meghaduta. Trans.: G. H. Rooke. Oxford, 1935.

One does indeed find many poems about love and women in Chinese poetry, but the tenor is completely different—sighs for unrequited love, complaints of unfaithfulness, sorrow at the lot of women, admiration of a woman's spiritual qualities, her learning, her grace, and modesty. It is, of course, dangerous to select poems for comparison, but it is interesting to compare a typical Chinese poem of about the same time, about a boy and girl sent to gather rushes for thatching.

> *'Green rushes with red shoots,*
> *Long leaves bending to the wind—*
> *You and I in the same boat,*
> *Plucking rushes at the Five Lakes.*
> *We started at dawn from the orchard-island:*
> *We rested under the elms till noon.*
> *You and I plucking rushes,*
> *Had not plucked a handful when night came!'★*

Plucking the Rushes: Anonymous. Trans.: Arthur Waley.

These two equally charming poems illustrate the difference in spirit which animates the two national geniuses.

The frank Indian descriptions of female beauty resulted in a vocabulary of ideal beauty—slim waists, full breasts, heavy hips, arched eyebrows, lips like fruit, etc. Nor did the call to religious life necessarily deprive the worshipper of sensual pleasures. They were merely transferred to paradise and he was asked to forgo the pleasure of women on earth for the infinitely more seductive pleasures of the heavenly maidens, more beautiful and more desirable than any woman on earth. The classic illustration of this concerns a certain Nanda, younger brother of the Buddha, whose desirable wife so filled his thoughts that he could not give up his life to follow the Buddha. The Buddha, according to the story, took him to heaven and showed him the delights of the *apsaras*, and with this promise of eternal bliss before him, he was able to put the distracting thoughts of his beloved wife out of his mind and devote himself whole-heartedly to the service of the Buddha.

The concept of sensual bliss as the reward for virtuous devotion on earth had no parallel in Chinese thought before the introduction of Buddhism. The female aspect of the gods meant little to the Chinese. There is no Chinese parturition myth, nor after Shang times much emphasis on fertility. The Chinese had no cult of the Great Mother, the supra-mundane source of the universe and all its creatures; they had no cult of the womb, whereas this is among the most ancient of Indian beliefs dating back to before Āryan times when it had already become a personification of the life-force of the cosmos and all its beings. By the 7th century BC the Mother Goddess had been incorporated into the predominantly male deities of the Āryans as the one who really understood the secret hidden life-force of the universe by which all things are accomplished. In this respect Japan, which had these features in its early civilization, is closer in feeling to India than is China and the sensual aspects of Indian art found in the Japanese a more sympathetic response. The sensual and the erotic seems to come naturally to the Japanese. This is not to say that the Chinese were not attracted by the idea of sensual bliss, but one has the feeling that it embarrassed them. They were prepared to accept descriptions of physical features, especially, for instance, those concerning the Buddha's body, and they tried to interpret them in sculpture but they could not accept the full Indian ideals of female beauty. The anatomical completeness of, say, the figures of the Sanchi railings, is inconceivable in Chinese sculpture. Indeed it is possible to claim that the ripe fullness of the Indian ideal female form meant nothing to the slim, less endowed Chinese. To them it would have appeared foreign, unnatural and perhaps simply gross.

Plate 156

This fundamental difference in outlook shows itself immediately in Chinese Buddhist sculpture. Where an unclothed figure is intended in the earliest period, the anatomical details are either treated cursorily or completely ignored. Always masters of the flat plane and the flowing lines of drapery the Chinese artists rapidly clothed their figures in heavy all-enveloping robes whose folds were beautifully arranged. It is significant that it took the Chinese less than half a century at Yün-kang to work this major change on an art of which they had hitherto had no experience.

It took them the whole of the 6th century to become accustomed to the idea of revealing parts of the body in a natural manner and to depicting their gods in recognizably human form. This relaxation can be seen in the Mai-chi-shan caves. It took again the full and direct impact of the greatest period of Indian sculpture, that of the Gupta centuries, to enable the Chinese to imbue their sculpture with a modified sensuality.

Plate 150

When the T'ang dynasty (618–907) firmly established itself in China conditions changed radically. China was powerful and confident after centuries of division and political uncertainty. Her armies controlled Central Asia and the traffic to and from India was intensified. From this strength and confidence came tolerance and intellectual curiosity. Buddhism was by now completely accepted and the first shock of Indian frankness in art had worn off. The Chinese began to realize the full plastic possibilities of the human form. Central Asia no longer played the important part it had hitherto done in the transmission and modification of Indian art forms. The two cultures were close together and Chinese pilgrims were writing first-hand reports of India and its products.

At the same time China itself was enjoying a period of great wealth and luxury, and this helped to make sensual themes more readily acceptable than hitherto, particularly in art and in poetry. The poet debauched with wine and women became an accepted literary personality.

In India, from the 4th century AD to the early T'ang period a great empire, that of the Guptas, was producing some of the finest sculpture in its history. The Gupta kings rapidly established an empire which by about AD 400 included all but the south of the sub-continent. The Chinese traveller Fa-hsien commented on the peace and order of the land. This empire was weakened by an invading nomad people from Central Asia, but was restored for a brief period by King Harṣa (reigned 606–647), during whose reign the second great Chinese pilgrim Hsüan-tsang visited India. Its sculpture has been summarized by Goetz as 'the collective product of the poets and priests who provided the imagery, of the actress-hetairae who explored the potentialities of expression through the medium of the human body, and lastly of the sculptors who had a perfect knowledge of anatomy, but could never regard that latter as a means of expression by itself'.* The style was basically the consummation of that of Mathurā but immeasurably enriched by a multitude of divinities and religious imagery.

The rhythm and balanced poses of these sculptures owe much to the influence of the dance in which every gesture and position of head, arms, hands, feet, neck and eyes have their own significance. What poetry was to the Chinese painter, dancing was to the Indian sculptor—the basic reference material of his art. The result was an art in which the desire to express physical beauty and controlled energy sustained nearly three centuries of lyrical inspiration.

Mention of the influence of the dance on sculpture naturally leads to the problem of the *mudrās* or hand gestures. They began about the time of Christ when images of the Buddha were first made and in the early period, up to about the 8th century, they symbolically recalled episodes taken from the Buddhist legends. However, these gestures were not Buddhist inventions for they had already passed through a long formative period and must equally owe a great deal to gestures of the dance. In fact the relationship of iconography and dance poses must be extremely ancient and close. The Gandhāra school exploited this repertoire of gestures, added them to the anthropomorphic forms of Greek and Roman sculpture and thus introduced them into Central Asia and finally into the Far East. As used in China in the first period of Buddhist sculpture they were interpreted somewhat loosely. Towards the

*H. Goetz: op. cit.

3   GUARDIAN FIGURE in painted clay. Tun-huang, Kansu province (8th century).

4

8th century AD, Tantric Buddhism, a combination of Yogic practices and mahāyāna theories, reached its full development. Magic formulae played a large part in the teachings of Tantric Buddhism, and the simple hand gestures which once referred to legend gained infinite mystical and magical powers. Through them the worshipper could achieve identity with the Supreme Unity. The number of *mudrās* rapidly developed into hundreds, but for the early period of Buddhist sculpture only about fifteen are of importance.*

E. Dale Saunders: *Mudrā*. New York, 1960.

When the left hand is turned downwards with palm exposed, it indicates that the Buddha will fulfil all vows and symbolizes his charity. The right hand raised with palm exposed, is a gesture familiar in western as well as eastern sculpture and in Buddhist thought indicates the desire to reassure or grant freedom from fear. A legend tells of how an enemy of the Buddha caused an elephant to become drunk and as he was about to trample the Buddha, he raised his right hand in this gesture and thus immediately stopped and calmed the maddened beast. This was the most popular gesture for Buddhas from about AD 460 to 750.

The gesture in which the right hand rests on the right knee with palm turned inwards as if touching the ground comes from a legend in which the Buddha, challenged by the king of demons, called upon the gods of the earth to destroy these evil spirits. An alternative version of the story is that, in his dispute with the king of evil for the throne of knowledge, the Buddha, who had no troops of demons to support his claim, touched the earth to act as witness to his right. This gesture dispersed Mara's army.

When the two hands are shown one upon the other in the lap, the gesture indicates the *mudrā* of concentration. It symbolizes the intense meditation by means of which the worshipper hopes to identify himself with the Supreme Unity. Legend has it that this was the attitude the Buddha took when he sat under the Bodhi tree during his last night of meditation. He moved from this position to touch the earth to call on it to testify to his triumph over the forces of evil. More generally it indicates the Buddhist qualities of tranquillity, impassivity and aloofness.

To end these very brief remarks on the basic iconography of Buddhist statues one should mention the lotus. Flowers play a large part in Indian religious thought and the lotus was popular before Buddhism took it over as a particularly meaningful

4 GUARDIAN FIGURES in painted clay. Cave of the Thousand Buddhas, Tun-huang, Kansu province.

symbol. It is the symbol of spontaneous generation and therefore, when used as the throne on which the Buddha sits, it indicates his divine birth. It grows from the mud at the bottom of a pond to blossom above the water in the purest of colours. Thus also the Buddha was born in the world but rose above it, surpassing it and unaffected by it. A Buddhist is said to represent a lotus when he is born and his life is like that of the flower as it withers and fades. It came to signify summer and spiritual and material strength and finally in Tantric Buddhism it came to represent the female principle and the female sexual organ. First used in Gandhāran sculpture, it spread throughout the mahāyānist world and sculptors found it particularly suitable as a seat for Buddhist statues since it was easily adapted to any size of pedestal.

The westerner, faced with a multiplicity of similar images, may be somewhat overwhelmed by the seemingly repetitive nature of Buddhist sculpture, especially in the early periods. However, it must be remembered that the Buddhist sculptor was not expected to create a work of art which in any way expressed his own personal view of the divinity. He was required to create devotional images which at best remained as close as possible to the original and at least incorporated a number of features which by tradition distinguished the Buddha's physical appearance. These features tended to curb any tendency which may have existed to impart originality of execution to religious icons, and in the early centuries would tend to make changes in style very difficult. The demands of iconographic accuracy were supported by the popular belief that the closer a statue was to its original, the more of the original's magic power it thus preserved. According to literary sources the early missionaries and their Chinese converts set up statues which stayed as close as possible to originals which in turn had been brought to China from Central Asian centres like Kucha, or even from India itself.

This held true for the earliest period and down to about the end of the 5th century and above all for images of Sākyamuni, the Historical Buddha. However, when other Buddhas, whose attributes were less circumscribed by tradition, displaced Sākyamuni, the sculptors obviously felt more free to interpret them according to their own ideas and those of the period. At all times they tended to rely on the written word or on sketches brought back by travellers and these were open to individual interpretation. Artistic conventions and rigid formulae invariably produce a reaction and there is plenty of evidence that the arrival of a new statue created considerable excitement. When left to themselves the sculptors were able to create, as for instance in the Lung-mên style, a manner which was completely Chinese and owed very little to outside influences.

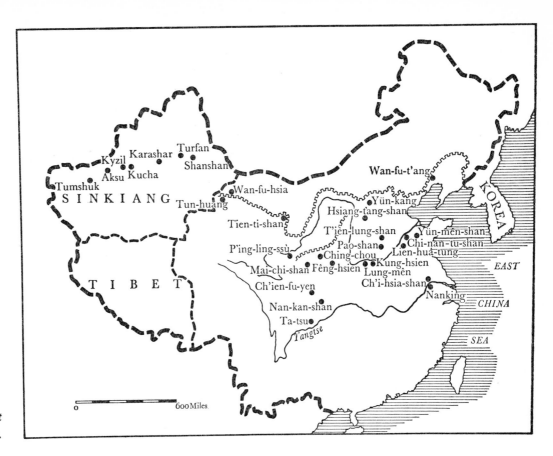

2　*Distribution of Buddhist cave-temple sites.*

The history of Chinese Buddhist sculpture, especially in the period up to about AD 450, is likely to remain vague and fragmentary in the extreme. The explorers of Central Asia at the beginning of this century discovered many remains of Buddhist centres like Kucha, but, as Mizuno admits, we still know little about the actual relationships existing between India, Central Asia and China during this early period.* Nor, despite a mass of material, do we understand the development of Gandhāran sculpture and its relationship with the sculpture of Bāmiyān—both key regions in north India from which the artistic trail leads through Central Asia to China. The oases in Central Asia, once thriving centres of the faith, have indeed yielded a great deal of material, but little of it is accurately dated and much work remains to be done on the two-way exchange of art and culture in this vast area. Most of the evidence we have of the earliest styles comes from small portable bronzes.

The arrival and first centuries of the Buddhist religion in China are hardly better documented. Buddhism probably first entered China at about the time of Christ, and historical sources refer to Buddhist practices and monuments there soon after.

S. Mizuno: *Bronze and Stone Sculpture of China*. Tokyo, 1960. *Plates 142, 143, 146*

Plates 144, 145

31

The Chinese possibly first started to make Buddhist images about AD 200 hardly distinguishing the foreign from the native divinities, but none of these have survived. The earliest surviving images of Buddha figures are found on the backs of bronze mirrors and as applied plaques on ceramic vessels of a type called *yüeh*. It is probable that actual sculptures were also being made at this time though none have survived.

The earliest Chinese Buddhist statue to survive dates from about AD 300, a bodhisattva in bronze 33.3 inches in height in the Fujii Collection, Kyōto, and this is the most close to the Gandhāra style of a number of bronze statues of the 4th century. The features and dress of the other statuettes show a formalization and modifications on the western style which reflect the growing influence of native Chinese taste and artistic traditions. For instance the hair is less naturalistically treated than in the Fujii statue, the robes are reduced to more simple patterns of looped folds and the features begin to lose their western cast. In doing so they become more mask-like.

The early 5th-century bronzes are, in the main, a continuation of the 4th-century styles supported by more skilful casting techniques. However, the dress shows an increased tendency towards stylization and the features grow softer and more expressionful than hitherto. New elements, presumably from Central Asia, began to influence the bronze sculptors—especially in the middle of the century when the artists began to treat the robes as integral parts of the bodies they cover, allowing contours of thighs and abdomen to show through, at times quite clearly.

During the second half of the 5th century, the period of the Yün-kang Caves, the styles of the late 4th–early 5th century were steadily developed and mastered. From about AD 477 heavy Chinese style robes cover the figures, revealing part of the right shoulder. These native type robes show the body beneath them in a manner inspired by Indian practices but modified by the art of the Central Asian oases.

Plates 153, 157

The move of the capital to Loyang in AD 494 was the ultimate political recognition of a process of sinicization which had been working strongly on the northern tribes. In art this change was expressed from the late 5th century onwards by the most radical change in style that Chinese sculpture had experienced. Quite suddenly it seems, the heavy full figures became slender and almost cylindrical. The faces were conceived in less plastic terms, long, sharply cut faces with angular chins surmounted elongated tube-like necks. The sculptors who had hitherto been familiarizing themselves with warm treatment of the flesh beneath their robes suddenly hid all traces of physical features beneath voluminous dress. Bachhofer describes the rhythms of this new dress as 'cataracts of sharply cut pleats'.* The poses are stiff and

L. Bachhofer: *A Short History of Chinese Art.* New York, 1946.

formalized. The archaic smile is retained, but it now contributed to the most spiritual expression that Chinese sculpture ever achieved. This most distinctive style, certainly the most 'Chinese' of all, prevailed over the whole of China until the period of 535–550 when the figures became less tense and new canons began to influence the sculptors.

From the mid-6th century the Chinese began to visualize their deities and those who served them in human form giving the bodies warm natural contours and the faces a new worldly tenderness. Figures were now free standing in the round, the right shoulder completely uncovered and the lips for the first time take their natural shape. The archaic smile has disappeared in the effort to give life to stone. The static quality of the typical early 6th-century Lung-mên style began to break down and the traditional Chinese emphasis on line and outline began to disappear. Jewellery appears as the foil to the body surfaces. Such figures show an early effort to bring flow and movement through the *tribhanga,* or thrice-bent, movement of the body which is so typical of the now powerful Gupta influences. *Plate 151*

The unification of China in 589 was the signal for a tremendous increase in Buddhist activity of all kinds, and sculpture shared the prosperity of the faith. The style of the Sui dynasty, about 600, forms the link between the pre-T'ang and full T'ang styles. The figures are heavier and fuller than in the mid-6th century and often richly adorned. The flesh of the large works often shows a smooth delicacy and the drapery, sometimes heavy, is always sensitively expressed. The faces are full and carry one stage further the Chinese sculptors' search for ideal beauty to be achieved in the full T'ang style. The increasing influence of Indian styles is even more visible in minor figures where the restraint demanded of the main icons is less evident.

Finally in the T'ang dynasty (618–907) the full and direct impact of Indian art reached China. The works of the period are the complete expression of the urbane, sophisticated and worldly life of this society. In the first period lingering influences *Plate 152* of the Sui modes persist, but soon the bodies became softer, more delicate and lithe. *Plate 154* Drapery flows, facial expressions are benign and the general effect is one of intimacy with the gods. The sculptors now seem fully to have understood the human organism and gave their deities figures of clear articulation, balanced and natural rhythms, and relaxed gentle movement. The full relaxation and elegance is seen in the figures of T'ien-lung-shan and P'ing-ling-ssŭ. A new sensitivity appears in these *Plate 154* figures which, at its finest, is combined with an imposing majesty. The tendency further towards naturalism increased in the late 7th–early 8th centuries and can be seen in the 8th century *arhats* on the walls of the K'an-ching-ssŭ at Lung-mên. Some of the late T'ang figures are so completely human that they seem to lose their divine character. The Indian style is acting directly on the Chinese and being assimilated and re-interpreted to serve the whole of the Far East.

The Sung period took on the voluptuousness of the T'ang but deprived it of its majesty. The mood changed from one of supra-human beauty to very human elegance, from divine to worldly royalty. This loss of the divine quality was irreparable, and sincere craftsmen could only seek higher qualities in guardian figures and in portrait sculpture.

The non-Buddhist sculpture of the Ming period—as seen in the tombs of the emperors at Nanking and near Peking—seems to disregard the lessons learnt from Buddhist sculpture during the preceeding thousand years and returns to the traditions of the Han dynasty, producing immobile and heavy figures, the surfaces of the stone blocks worked in beautiful detail. Though such monoliths may well suit the art of a tomb they impress mainly by their size and setting.

Chinese sculpture atrophied rapidly from the beginning of the Ming dynasty at the end of the 14th century. It is just as difficult to produce reasons for the decline of late sculpture at it is to understand how a second-rate Hellenism in Gandhāra inspired the Chinese to the masterpieces of the 5th–6th centuries. The heavy, immobile Ming tomb figures are almost as far removed from the T'ang litheness and movement as are the Han guardians of five hundred years before them. When the tree of Buddhism died in India from the 10th century onwards, the branch in China seems also to have withered and no fresh inspiration came to take its place.

After the Sung dynasty intelligent Chinese seem to have transferred their interest to the revived Confucianism. The Mongol invasion seems to have broken the tradition of religious statuary in stone. Much of the early work was the direct result of imperial patronage, but from the Ming dynasty onwards the court transferred its financial support from Buddhism to Confucianism too. Architecture profited at the expense of sculpture. Sculptural skills henceforward turned to modelling, notably in the Fukien ceramic *blanc-de-chine* figures, in which the accumulated skills of the past thousand years found new expression. The monumental art of China found outlets in architecture. The magnificent Buddhist interlude was over.

1 ARCHAIC ART: BRONZES AND JADES

FEW ancient civilizations have yielded their treasures so wantonly but their secrets so unwillingly as that of China. The museums of the world contain magnificent collections of early Chinese art, especially bronzes, but serious archaeological work only began less than forty years ago to ascertain how they were made and the circumstances of their burial. Only in the last ten years have scholars, through scientific excavation, discovered the keys to some of the problems of China's earliest periods.

The culture of this ancient civilization in the post-Neolithic period, that is to say for about the first fifteen hundred years until the time of Christ, is distinguished by two remarkable arts—those of bronze and jade. Chinese civilization developed in comparative isolation in the far east of the Asiatic mainland, and the early Chinese discovered and perfected the difficult skills required for fashioning these materials into objects of great artistic beauty.

The earliest Chinese dynasty of which we have any definite knowledge is that generally known as the Shang dynasty which was paramount in central China c. 1523–1028 BC. The magnificent bronzes which are the pride of many western collections were mostly made in the second half of this period when the capital of their state was situated at An-yang, an easily defendable site on a bend of the Yellow River. They are the products of an already highly developed civilization whose people lived in fine houses. An extensive artisan and peasant class supported a leisured nobility whose activities were recorded by skilled scribes.

Bronze vessels were buried with important persons and formed an indispensible part of ancester worship, the main religious activity of the early Chinese. Although made in moulds, by relatively crude methods, their shapes are powerful and varied, the finish is of rare perfection, and although the decoration is intricate, the general effect is of overwhelming strength. Powerful, almost sinister, expressions of the spirit, these objects, both large and small, have an unmistakable unity of style. They testify to a highly disciplined religion and way of life.

It is obvious that such bronzes marked a very advanced stage of bronze manufacture. Until recently their pre-An-yang inspiration was totally obscure. So much so that some scholars were led to the conclusion that this was a cultural achievement which must have been introduced in larger or smaller degree from the west. However, since the last war, archaeological work under the Communist régime has been greatly intensified. One of the major discoveries has been that of the site of the Shang capital prior to that of An-yang. This was the site near the modern city of Chêng-chou, some 200 miles south of An-yang. In the remains of this ancient city of Ao were unearthed more humble predecessors of the technically and artistically perfect bronzes of late Shang times. The shapes are less varied, the decoration simpler and more restrained, the workmanship crude in comparison with late Shang. The culture of Chêng-chou clearly sprang from neolithic antecedents of Shang and bronze appears for the first time only in its second level. We do not know how the Chinese first made the discovery of bronze, but almost certainly it was made by the Chinese independently and, once learned, was rapidly carried to magnificent heights.

As the Shang Chinese grew in strength so their art increased in richness and the area they controlled expanded. Their invention of the chariot and the development of refined weapons increased their skill in warfare. Bronze was used for fittings and weapons, and all show the same accomplishment. They carried out raids on their less advanced neighbours, enslaved their captives and not infrequently immolated them in the tombs of the great. Their palaces on the surface were matched by immense tombs under the earth which have yielded countless treasure (most of it to pillage). The Shang developed a social organization on a feudal system which was elaborated in the successive centuries and ruled an expanding China for the following thousand years. The Chinese owe to the Shang peoples one of the most important cultural discoveries—that of writing.

By the second half of the Shang dynasty Chinese writing was already at a comparatively advanced stage, and had reached a form which it was to preserve for the next thousand years. Scholars have concluded that writing of a primitive type must have existed in neolithic times, but the refined civilization of Shang demanded a script capable of considerable flexibility and nuance. The vast majority of early inscriptions are incised on bone or cast in metal, but a few brush written characters have survived. From the Han dynasty onwards calligraphy rapidly developed into an art closely allied to and as respected as painting. New forms of the characters were invented and the works of the great masters were closely studied. It is no exaggeration to say that calligraphy is one of the basic ingredients of the Chinese aesthetic, and much of the vitality of Chinese painting springs from their constant search for life, balance and beauty of line in this most abstract of all arts.

To return to the bronzes, their most striking aspect is their decoration. This is a combination of geometric patterns and highly formalized animal forms. The origin of this animal decoration is not clear. When it occurs on the earliest bronzes it is already highly stylized. Animal hunts formed an important part of the life of the Shang nobility, both for sport and military training, and the animals and man's power over them must have inspired the Chinese artist as it did the artists of many early societies. The animals are often of terrifying mien and the art itself is of an awesome rather than a purely decorative quality. As the bronzes are objects of religious import, the decorations are most likely to be mystical symbols. As objects to be used in offerings to the ancestors or as rewards for the highest achievements they must have produced reactions of the profoundest respect. The force and energy of the Shang people speaks in all their work. In the later Shang work the decoration often fills every piece of the surface of the vessel and sometimes even seems to expand outwards explosively from their surfaces. An effective dichotomy is visible in all early bronzes: barbarity and refinement, elaboration and severity, abandon and discipline, delicacy and grossness, sheer animal vigour and elegance. Within a limited repertoire, the variety is unlimited. A supreme confidence inspires every line.

The fate which overtook the Shang dynasty set the pattern for many dynasties during succeeding centuries. The Chou, a more vigourous tribe, akin to them in race, gained strength from its need to defend itself against more primitive peoples on its borders. Envious of the wealth of its seigneurs the Shang, it finally took possession of Shang lands and overlordship. The Chou dynasty thus established lasted, according to the official chronologies, from about 1027 BC to 256 BC. However, the real power of the Chou kings lasted only until about 771 BC. From then onwards the growing power of the feudal lords gave them virtual independence and the Chou authority survived in name only. The feudal lords accepted it because none of them was sufficiently strong to assume overall kingship. The Chou moved their capital from An-yang to the safer area of the east. The second half of the Chou reign is itself divided into two, known as the Spring and Autumn era (772–481 BC) from the title of the annals of the state of Lu, Confucius' state, which cover that period, and the Warring States period (480–221 BC) whose name speaks for itself. These centuries of violent internecine struggle culminated in the supremacy of one of the states, that of Ch'in, which defeated all its rival states and unified the country. Warfare changed from being an aristocratic pastime in which chivalry and magnanimity marked the behaviour of victor to vanquished, to a bloody fight for survival.

At the same time China was expanding rapidly. Land and the people it could support were the symbols of real wealth. Luxuries like bronze, once reserved for the kings and nobles, became available to a wider segment of society. The centuries of military and political upheaval stimulated men to think deeply and passionately about the fundamental problems of life, and, as described in the Introduction, the outcome of this period of intense intellectual activity was the so-called 'Hundred Schools of Philosophy'. Confucianism is the best known of these since, after a long struggle, it eventually emerged victorious. Yet at this time it nearly perished at the hands of more violent creeds such as that which brought the State of Ch'in to power, and not till many centuries after the death of its founder did Confucianism triumph.

The Chou were obviously great admirers of the Shang people they conquered, for they at first accepted its art wholesale. Thus it is extremely difficult to distinguish bronzes made in the first century of Chou rule from those made earlier. Then some of the Shang shapes disappear from the bronze workers' repertoire, and animal forms either lose favour completely or are treated more decoratively than in earlier works. In the 5th century another major change took place, which strangely enough brought back into favour some of the Shang motifs—though again treated more decoratively. New centres of bronze manufacture throughout the country produced works with strong local characteristics.

For the first time in this period the art of the nomad peoples of the Ordos region began to influence the bronze designer directly. Together with the more free and fanciful use of traditional motifs, an increasing love of animals, which characterizes the art of nomad peoples, affected Chinese art. Although from earliest times examples of naturalistic animals exist in Chinese art, henceforward they dominate. The departure of the *t'ao-t'ieh* animal mask in this period takes with it much of the mystery of early Chinese art, a mystery largely still not solved.

The nomad peoples, like the pre-Columbian Americans, provide many intriguing problems. These people of the Eurasian steppe, the Scythians and kindred tribes, occupied a vast area stretching from the western fringe of European Russia to the borders of China, a huge area of grassland cut by the Pamirs, the T'ien-shan range and the Altai mountains. Communications were difficult and especially so at the dawn of the historic period when deserts formed in Central Asia, but they seem to have remained fairly effective. The origins of these people are obscure, but most scholars believe that the nomad tribes, all of whom spoke a common Iranian tongue and enjoyed a similar art, were either of Indo-European origin or emerged from the Altai region of Central Asia itself. There was a certain Mongoloid admixture, probably through inter-marriage. The most important of them were certainly the Scythians, a term used sometimes for many of these nomad peoples but by Russian scholars for those who lived in the area of the Sea of Azov, the Black Sea, the Kuban and the banks of the Oxus. There is much evidence to support the fact that these tribes originated in the western Siberia area. Certainly they came into contact with China very early in Chinese history and it was a Chinese campaign *c.* 800 BC against one of the tribes, the Hsiung-nu, a constant threat to the more settled people in the south, which drove this tribe to the west and caused a violent unsettling of populations right across Central Asia and into Europe.

Living in an area which teemed with game, hunting seems to have been the principal economic activity and sport of the nomads. They were so absorbed by the activities of the world of the animals that, as Tamara Talbot Rice says, 'The tribes-men developed an acute awareness of the beast world and a far more profound understanding of it than many of us can today realize'.* The nomads lived, if not a comfortable, at least a basically adventurous life and produced an exciting art. The ancient Chinese also loved the chase and no doubt learned much from the nomadic tribesmen, for both used it as a preparation for war. Art influences must have travelled wider and faster than we sometimes imagine. For instance in the famous frozen tombs of Pazirik (5th century BC) were found among other things Chinese textiles and a carpet, now in the Hermitage Museum, Leningrad, which may have come from Persia and is certainly the oldest in the world.

The Scythians. London, 1957.

In the art of the nomads, as also in Chinese art, man played very little part. The bronze in *plates 14, 15 and 16* is one of the very few Chinese bronzes in which man appears and the meaning of his appearance there completely escapes us. Almost invariably in nomadic art the animal dominates—particularly the stag, eagle and a number of strange griffin-like creatures of the imagination. Leopards spring on stags, their mortal combats caught in magnificent silhouettes. The people of the Altai region were at the height of their power in the 4th–3rd centuries BC and the Chinese seem to have found the vitality, movement and barbarity of their art irresistible. Its full power reached China when the inspiration which had created the early bronzes was on the wane and it reinvigorated an art which had lasted with diminishing power for over a thousand years. The emotional and rhythmic effect of nomad art, to say nothing of its naturalism, seems to have opened up a completely new field of artistic experience to the Chinese of the time. One of the most prevalent and mystifying aspects of this northern art—the use of the antler—profoundly influenced Chinese and Korean art, though again its meaning remains obscure.

If bronze is not a characteristic of Chinese civilization at all ages, jade certainly is. Only the Maoris of New Zealand and the Indians of pre-Columbian South America realized its possibilities, appreciated its beauty, and developed the difficult skills necessary to work it. The Chinese produced incomparably the finest works of art in jade and built up a whole symbolism attached to it. The moral qualities which we attribute to the diamond and the pearl, the Chinese see in jade—purity, steadfastness, beauty, integrity.

Its use was fairly widespread for simple decorations and for tools throughout the main neolithic cultures of China. The white jade, always considered the finest, was brought from Central Asia or from Siberia, which again underlines the Chinese debt to the nomad peoples and the close contacts with nomad areas even in the very earliest times.

In Shang times jade was used generally for small objects, for pendants usually in the shape of fish and animals, for hairpins, ritual weapons such as dagger axes, for objects of practical use such as handles for implements and arrow heads, for an interesting group of objects, discs with a hole in the centre or squared tubes, of which the precise signification or use is unknown. The thin flat blades of dagger axes are beautifully smooth and have a strange ominousness. The tendency is towards a greater use of jade for decorative purposes and so to a greater use of decoration on them. On the whole the decorative techniques of Shang jade carving are crude. Some of the small pendants have the same monumental quality that distinguishes almost every part of the bronzes. Human figures occur in jades. Unfortunately long burial has resulted in the calcification of many Shang jades with a resultant loss of the lustre which contributes to their beauty and tactile attraction. But by the time of the Warring States and Han the conquest of technical or artistic problems was complete and the art of jade carving acquired the quality of jewellery which was to be preserved for the following two thousand years.

Notes on the plates on page 49

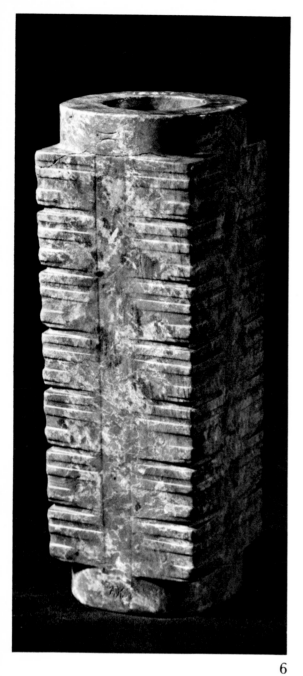

6

8

7

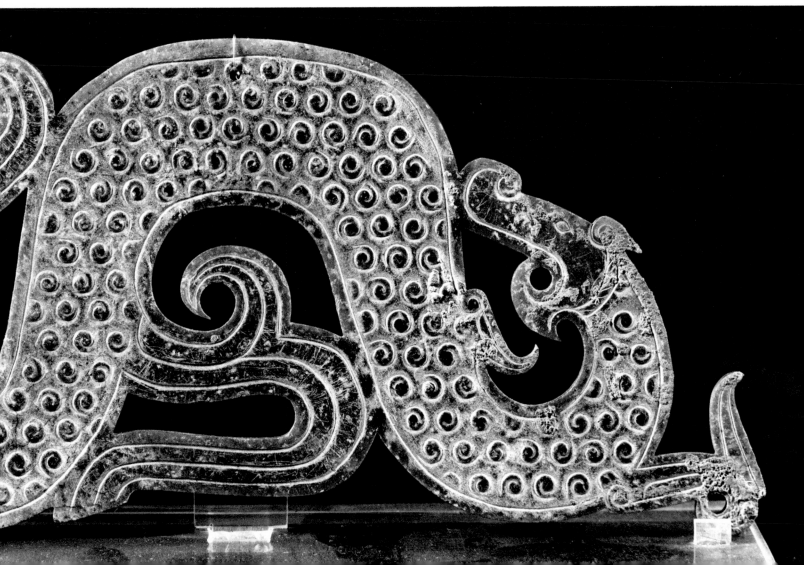

13

14

15

16

NOTES ON THE PLATES TO CHAPTER I

5   POLE TERMINAL in the form of the head of a *t'ao-t'ieh* monster, in bronze. Shang dynasty (*c.* 1500–1027 BC). Height 18 cm (7¹/₈″). *Musée Cernuschi, Paris.*

6   JADE RITUAL IMPLEMENT, *ts'ung*, a hollow tube, known later as a symbol of the earth. Warring States period (481–221 BC). *Musée Guimet, Paris.*

7   BRONZE TIGER from the Ordos region. Length 10 cm (4″). *Musée Guimet, Paris.*

8   BRONZE TIGER from the Ordos region. Length 14 cm (5¹/₂″). *Musée Cernuschi, Paris.*

9   WHITE JADE TIGER of the Han dynasty (206 BC–AD 220). Length 19 cm (7¹/₂″). *Musée Guimet, Paris.*

10   WHITE JADE DRAGON of the Warring States period (481–221 BC). Length 19 cm (7¹/₂″). *Musée Guimet, Paris.*

11   BRONZE MONSTER MASK of the mid-Chou dynasty (8th–6th centuries BC). *Musée Guimet, Paris.*

12   BRONZE APPLIQUÉ in the form of a serpent. Warring States period (481–221 BC). Diam. 22.8 cm (9″). *Musée Guimet, Paris.*

13   COVER OF A RITUAL BRONZE vessel, type *kuang*. Shang dynasty (*c.* 1500–1027 BC). Height 23 cm (9¹/₈″). *Freer Gallery of Art, Washington D.C.*

14   TIGRESS AND HUMAN FIGURE—bronze ritual vessel, type *yu*. Shang dynasty (*c.* 1500–1027 BC). Height 35 cm (14″). *Musée Cernuschi, Paris. See p. 39.*

15   Front view of *plate 14.*

16   Back view of *plate 14.*

17   ELEPHANT—bronze ritual vessel, type *tsun*. Early Chou dynasty (11th–9th centuries BC). *Musée Guimet, Paris.*

II THE GREAT WALL AND THE SCULPTURES OF THE HAN DYNASTY

THE Great Wall of China is without doubt the greatest monument that a nation ever created to mark its unification. In the two thousand two hundred years which have passed since it was built, many of the finest monuments of this prolific people have been destroyed. Sculptures in stone have decayed, great bronzes have been melted down, temples have vanished in religious persecutions or natural disasters. But the Great Wall remains, crumbling here and there, pierced many times, eroded by wind and rain, robbed of some of its stones and bricks, so that in places even its course is difficult to trace. Nevertheless hundreds of miles of this huge rampart still define China's old northern frontier. Starting at the sea in the east, it travels 1,500 miles to the mountains in the west, a huge rampart of stone, brick and earth with fortresses every 200 yards along its length. It crosses a formidable terrain with complete disregard for natural features, clinging to the crests of steep hills, blocking the passes, leaping rivers, crossing deserts—'the supreme monument to the engineering courage of ancient China'.★ At its lowest point, the Wall is 80 feet below sea level, at its highest point it rises to 10,000 feet. In many places 30 feet wide at its base, on its top three people could ride abreast or in ancient times chariots could pass. The vastness of the project has inspired some unusual statistics. One early writer who journeyed its entire length estimated that the material it contains would build a wall 3 feet thick and 8 feet high round the equator, and even more strange, that it is perhaps the only man-made object on the face of the earth which could be seen from the moon. In reality it overwhelms the imagination for it crosses one-twentieth of the world's circumference, and would be thus the equivalent of a rampart running from Paris to Istanbul or from London to Athens. Other nations well into modern times have dreamed of finding security behind a wall, but none have tried to realize their dreams so remorselessly and yet so vainly as the Chinese.

The Great Wall makes a clear historical as well as geographical division. When in the 3rd century BC Ch'in Shih Huang Ti, the First Emperor, united China and

W. E. Geil: *The Great Wall of China*. London, 1909.

completed the Wall, politically the country entered its 'modern' period. But a thousand years of recorded history lay behind this achievement, and to understand the military, political and psychological reasons for creating such a giant fortification, we must look briefly at some aspects of these earlier centuries.

The Shang, from their capital at An-yang on the Yellow River, controlled a relatively small area of China. Outside its loosely defined borders lay less developed states of kindred peoples whom the Shang seem sometimes to have victimized in raids for slaves and for prisoners to immolate in their royal graves. But the history and art of the Shang lie outside the period which led to the building of the Great Wall. It was not until the 10th century BC when the kindred Chou people from the west defeated and succeeded the Shang that China began rapidly to expand, to form new states to the north, south and east. The Chou created the idea of a community of independant states more or less civilized according to age and closeness to the centre, but all basically similar in culture and owing allegiance to the House of Chou.

From about the year 1000 BC the Chou kings exercised their power throughout civilized China through a feudal system. They were the political and religious heads of the country and the various feudal kings owed them allegiance. For nearly three centuries the Chou possessed the vigour which their frontier training had bred in them and they were able to maintain some authority over the various states. However, in 770 BC a people called the Ch'uang Jung sacked their capital and the Chou sought safety by moving their headquarters to the more settled, more secure eastern area. This retreat from the frontier marked the beginning of their loss of power and led to their final extinction some fifty years later. It is significant that the Ch'uang Jung were probably just that type of nomadic people whom the Chinese hoped to keep permanently at bay when they built the Great Wall. Thus the threat from the turbulent nomads in the north and west began to play its part in the political activities of China very early in its history.

From the time when the Chou established their capital at Lo-yang in Honan little by little they began to lose their power and authority. China was expanding rapidly, and the Chou were unable to control some of the new states being formed. The country became a loose confederation of some fifteen large states. The balance of power between these large states was delicate. None of them was strong enough to displace the Chou nor perhaps did they feel the necessity to do so. They may even have feared to remove them completely. Vestiges of the Chou power remained. They alone could ratify the lords in their feoffs and thus provide a steadying force in a period of increasing disorganization. Much of their authority derived also from the fact that they alone could perform the sacred ceremonies which, according to ancient Chinese belief, maintained the harmony of heaven and earth and ensured the prosperity of the four seasons. Politically, the feudal lords were independent in their territories and the urge to form larger political units was satisfied by the creation of hegemonies in which the most powerful lord of the time influenced the policy of a group of states.

The idea of aggrandisement at the expense of a weaker neighbour did not at first appeal to them. Independence and security of tenure seem to have been sacred concepts. Consequently warfare was a chivalrous affair, limited in scope and governed by strict rules. It seldom resulted in the disappearance of a state, however small.

However, towards the end of the period of the Spring and Autumn Annals, warfare began to take on a more serious aspect and become a matter of life and death. At first the large states swallowed their smaller neighbours, the anomalous enclaves disappeared and finally even the larger states were no longer safe in defeat. The centuries of the Warring States period (479–221 BC) saw the feudal system of ancient China completely broken down and the whole empire united under the ruthless control of the head of the state of Ch'in, Ch'in Shih Huang Ti, the First Emperor, as he entitled himself.

Ch'in State emerged in the west of China where it had gained and consolidated its strength by constant warfare with and indeed by assimilation of the more uncivilized peoples on its borders. The older Chinese states considered it a barbarian state. As these feudalities in the centre of China became increasingly enfeebled by their inter-state rivalries, Ch'in was able to expand steadily eastwards into the heart of the continent. By the 3rd century BC only six large states remained and these one by one fell to the assaults of the Ch'in. In 256 even the state of Chou was relieved of its last possessions and became extinct. In less than ten years between 230 and 222 BC the remaining states were overcome and Ch'in controlled the whole land.

Ch'in had adopted, characteristically, the ruthless Legalist doctrine and its principal propagator, a certain Wei Yang, lord of Shang, who said that man is fundamentally evil and must be strictly disciplined. To men of such a mind the theories of the other Hundred Schools of thought were, of course, extremely dangerous. When the state of Ch'in emerged supreme, it attempted to destroy all memory of them by proscribing their followers and burning their books. Much of the early writings of the Hundred Schools perished in this way, and it was only the efforts of Confucian scholars, when later they obtained power, that led to the recording and preservation of at least some of the Confucian works.

In their efforts to centralize the administration the Ch'in likewise aimed at eradicating in the general mind all memory of the existence of other states: therefore the written histories were put to the torch. The literary holocaust of 213 BC brought down the castigations of scholars in subsequent generations and made the name of Ch'in Shih Huang Ti among the most hated in China.

The First Emperor ruled a united China for only eleven years, but they were years packed with revolutionary changes in Chinese life. So complete and ruthless were his reforms that no matter how subsequent régimes condemned him they could never undo his work. He suppressed the various laws of the states and replaced them with those of Ch'in. He unified the weights, measurements and the system of tax collection. To facilitate communications and ease supply problems, the gauge of tracks for wagons was standardized. The writing of the Chinese language became standard throughout the empire and he thereby formed a unifying bond which has become ever stronger over the centuries. For, although Chinese in various areas speak completely different dialects, they can all read the same script. He collected all weapons not needed by the Ch'in armies and melted them down. The large militia of the independent states were demobilized and their energies directed into the cultivation of the land. For this reason, it must be admitted that later historians, almost exclusively Confucian, of course, have given him less credit than is really his due.

Once his domination of China was secure, he himself was free to direct his energies against the enemies threatening the land from without. His monument, the Great Wall, was intended as the foundation stone of a defensive system against the intrusions of the nomads of the Mongolian steppe. Ch'in Shih Huang Ti was not the first sovereign to conceive of such a defensive barrier and not all the present wall is his work. The Kings of Chao and Yen, whose states in Shansi and Hopei bordered the nomad country, had previously built shorter stretches of the wall, but he linked and extended it from the sea at Shan-hai-kuan in the east to the remote north-west frontier of his own state of Ch'in, a distance of 1,500 miles. Upon this stupendous construction tens of thousands of exiled criminals and others laboured ceaselessly under ruthless taskmasters. If the scholars of every succeeding century have cursed the name of the First Emperor for burning the books, popular tradition has held his memory in undying hatred for his methods of building the Wall. Even today, after more than two thousand years, the people repeat that a million men perished at the task and that every stone cost a human life. It may well be that the First Emperor saw in this vast undertaking and in similar projects such as the building of trunk roads not only

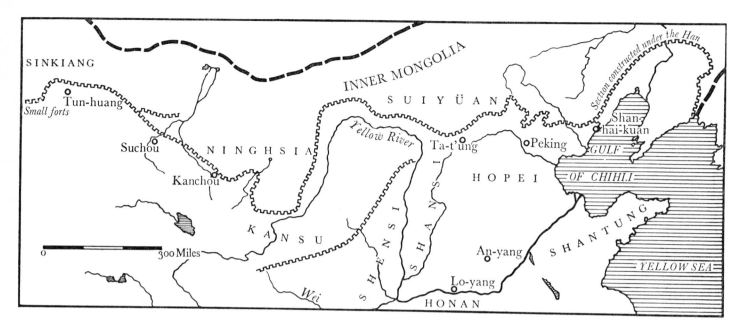

2 *The Great Wall.*

valid military projects, but also a means of absorbing the energies of a people long accustomed to almost continuous warfare.

The building of the Great Wall required such a prodigious effort that the Chinese must have estimated very highly the threat of the people it was intended to keep out. During Ch'in times there were three main nomadic peoples who threatened the Chinese. In the north-east were the Hou. The great Ch'in general, Mêng T'ien pushed them back from the bend in the Yellow River in 215 BC and in the following year started to build the part of the Wall which reached the sea in the east. Campaigning in the far west, he came into contact with the vigourous Tibetan tribes which occupied the mountainous valleys in the upper reaches of the Yellow River.

Translated by E. Chavannes as *Les Mémoires Historiques.* Paris, 1895–1905, 5 vol.

However, the main danger came from the people whom the Chinese called the Hsiung-nu and who came to be known in Europe as the Huns. According to Ssu-ma Ch'ien (*c.* 145–80 BC), who wrote the *Shih Chi**, the first history of China, these warlike people became a unified and strong nation for the first time towards the end of the 3rd century BC. In this they followed a pattern which subsequent northern tribes were later to follow. One great leader of a small tribe welded a number of kindred tribes into a national unit and organized a fast-moving fighting force which aimed at loot and conquest. China always offered particularly tempting possibilities. The most formidable of these alliances was of course that of the Mongols who established the Yüan dynasty in China in the 13th century.

54

The Huns were a group of peoples who had been living in the far east of Asia from at least the 2nd millennium BC. Their ultimate origins are unknown, and archaeological studies in the area, which would tell us much, have hardly begun. They absorbed a large amount of Mongolian blood and spoke an Ural-Altaic language. The Hsiung-nu were one tribe of this group and it was a great leader named Touman who united these peoples into a single empire which lasted for over 350 years from 209 BC to AD 160. The Chinese during the early years of the Chou dynasty had contacts with the northern tribes, ancestors of the Hsiung-nu. Diplomatic relations must have been frequent and Chinese refugees often sought asylum with these tribes who seem to have welcomed them. In the frontier areas, such as the state of Ch'in, relations must have been very close and the populations mixed. In succeeding centuries for long periods the Huns seem to have been serious rivals to the Chinese for political leadership and supremacy in the Far East. They were probably considerably more civilized than the Chinese would lead us to believe, and certainly their art influenced that of China from Han times or earlier. However, the Chinese wrote what historical records we have of the period and therefore they give a biased view of their activities and culture.

The Chinese respected them sufficiently to give Chinese maidens in marriage to their tribal chieftains. In 110 BC a Chinese princess named Hsi-chün was sent for political reasons to be the wife of a Central Asian nomad king. She found her husband old and decrepit. He only saw her once or twice a year, when they drank a cup of wine together. They could not converse as they had no language in common. Her lament has been translated by Arthur Waley:

> My people have married me
> In a far corner of Earth:
> Sent me away to a strange land,
> To the king of the Wu-sun.
> A tent is my house,
> Of felt are my walls;
>
> Raw flesh my food
> With mare's milk to drink.
> Always thinking of my own country,
> My heart sad within.
> Would I were a yellow stork
> And could fly to my old home!*

Arthur Waley: *170 Chinese Poems.* London, 1918, p. 53.

55

In 33 BC another Chinese girl named Chao-chün was given to the Khan of the Hsiung-nu and, according to tradition, her grave was the only place in this desolate country where grass would grow. The T'ang poet Po Chü-i in AD 809 wrote what is perhaps the saddest of these poems concerning the nomads. It tells how a Chinese living in the frontier areas was captured by the Tartars and forced to live with them for forty years. He was given a barbarian wife and had children by her. Finally the pull of his native land was too great and he escaped from his captors making his way painfully across the Gobi desert to the Chinese frontier. There, alack, he was again taken prisoner, this time by the Chinese who could not believe he was a genuine Chinese. With a group of other Tartar prisoners he was sent to forced labour in the south.

When I fell among Tartars and was taken prisoner, I pined for the land of Han:
Now that I am back in the land of Han, they have turned me into a Tartar.

★ ★ ★

Of all the sorrows of all the prisoners mine is the hardest to bear!
Never in the world has so great a wrong befallen the lot of man,—
A Han heart and a Han tongue set in the body of a Tartar.★

Ibid., pp. 127–130.

After the fall of the Han dynasty in AD 221 the Huns and allied peoples such as Turkomans were masters of all North China until AD 581. Under the powerful T'ang dynasty (AD 618–907), the Chinese were able to expel them from China proper, and to control much of Central Asia. With the fall of the T'ang, hordes of these people again invaded the Empire to such effect that during the whole period from AD 908 until the present day, native rulers have governed a united China for less than three hundred years. For the other seven hundred years of this millennium the Hunnish tribes have ruled either the whole of or large parts of China.

From early times, the movements of these nomad tribes of the Far East have affected the West. For example, these same peoples moved westwards, and in the 5th century AD the Persians were able to keep them at bay only by paying heavy tribute. The Turks, a kindred people, later occupied all of Persia and made themselves masters of the whole Near East. In the 5th and 6th centuries another band of Huns destroyed the glorious Gupta dynasty of India and, when the Turks adopted Islam, their campaigns led to their domination of India. They were only supplanted by the arrival of the British. Their effect on Europe was equally devastating. When the Chinese defeated them in the Far East, they turned westwards to displace other tribes living in Central Asia. The Gothic peoples who caused the premature downfall of the Roman Empire and terrified Europe were in fact little more than unhappy refugees, themselves fleeing from the onslaught of the even fiercer horsemen of the steppes pressing hard on their heels.*

W. M. McGovern: *The Early Empires of Central Asia.* U.S.A., 1939, pp. 87 ff.

Finally one must try to assess the value of the Great Wall in relation to these peoples. The Chinese certainly set great store by it, and from time to time, especially during the Ming dynasty (1368–1644), they extensively repaired it. However, it never permanently kept the nomads out. Its efficacy depended on its being adequately manned and, except for periods of great prosperity and effort, this proved to be impossible. The problems of supplying garrisons in its inhospitable area were so great that the Han emperors gave official titles to those who could arrange the transport of grain to the frontiers. Later, titles were sold to raise a fund for the same purpose. The Chinese records state that even criminals could gain remission of their terms of imprisonment if they were prepared to undertake the transport of grain. The difficulties of the Han emperors were increased by the lack of adequate means of transport. The northern border is ill-supplied with navigable rivers. The Yellow River itself flows southwards from the mountain plateau to the plains and transport barges had to make their way northward fully laden against the powerful stream and only gained the advantage of the current when returning empty. Horses were in short supply and had to be purchased or captured from the enemy.

The Chinese tried one obvious solution, that of trying to colonize the lands along the Wall. General Mêng T'ien settled 30,000 families to live on the Ordos plateau, the nomads' richest grazing area, but within a century the Hsiung-nu had taken the whole region. In 120 BC the Yellow River overflowed its banks flooding out some 700,000 farmers who were then settled in the Ordos region.

The Wall itself, when efficiently manned could be a considerable deterrent to raiding cavalry but it never did more than act as a line of demarcation between two entirely different types of civilization—the intensive settled agriculture of the south and the pastoral economy of the north. The pattern for the development of China was one of communities depending upon agriculture centred around walled cities. The natural extension of the walled city concept of society was the walled state and finally the walled nation. The Chinese type of agricultural economy, either 'wet' or 'dry', could expand easily towards the south, and this it did in subsequent centuries. What is more, the Chinese system of education bred administrators who understood the problems of governing this type of intensive agricultural state. The Wall turned the attentions of the Chinese towards the south. Beyond it lay areas which could not profitably be incorporated into China proper.

Thus the Wall remained obstinately the massive symbol of a no-man's-land. It demarcated an otherwise vague zone where one culture changed to another. Its area varied over the centuries according to the power of the peoples to the north and south of it. If the tribal penetrations became too deep, the invaders rapidly became sinicized—as with the Mongols and more recently the Manchus. If the Chinese ventured too far to the north they tended to become nomads. Thus, throughout the centuries, the area contained a whole range of groups ranging from sinicized nomads to semi-barbarous Chinese on the frontier, to the steppe peoples in Mongolia, the plateau people of Tibet and the various tribes of Turkestan. As the fortunes of China proper varied, so the different peoples this area contained tended to move either to the north or to the south.

The fundamental difference between the peoples of the north and south was that the former were seldom strong enough in resources and experience to create a settled empire without enlisting the support of the Chinese administrators, soon becoming Chinese themselves, whereas the Chinese at times of strength could always capture the oases of Turkestan and thus turn the Mongol flank. This was easier and more effective than manning the Great Wall. The Chinese, for their side, could never permanently end the ebb and flow of frontier peoples and maintain their civilization in that enclosed world which was the Chinese ideal.★ What has been called 'China's heroic effort to perfect her almost complete natural isolation'★ was in fact the greatest example of wasted military effort in the history of the world. Like so many defensive walls before and after it, it only created conditions in which those outside could build up their strength; it provided them with a permanent challenge to pierce it and lulled those whom it was supposed to protect into a sense of false security.

If one could judge the success of a ruler by his ability to make a nation willingly accept unpopular measures, the founders of the Ch'in dynasty would rank high among the world's politicians. When Ch'in Shih Huang Ti died, the Crown Prince was stationed at the Great Wall with the famous general Mêng T'ien. The Crown Prince, more liberal in outlook than his father, was in disgrace for disagreeing with the policy of burning the books. The ministers round the Emperor, on his death, feared for their positions, and their lives, if the Crown Prince came to the throne. They forged a letter purporting to be from the Emperor in which he ordered the Prince and the general to commit suicide. So great was their respect for Ch'in Shih Huang Ti and their fear of disobedience that they did not question the authenticity of the letter and duly killed themselves.

Owen Lattimore, 'Origins of the Great Wall of China', *The Geographical Review*, 1937, pp. 529–549.

G. B. Cressey: *China's Geographic Foundation.* U.S.A., 1934.

The ministers then placed the second son on the throne who was a man of little strength or capacity. The result was a reign of terror which lasted for only four years. The oppression from which the people suffered grew increasingly heavy, the forces of revolt gained strength from despair and finally a civil war broke out which swept away the Ch'in house, though not its considerable achievements. Thus fell a dynasty which its founder had hoped would last ten thousand generations.

The early Han emperors pursued and achieved the same objectives as the First Emperor but by more devious and skilful means. Their success was such that whereas under Ch'in Shih Huang Ti the majority of people considered the concept of a united China as alien and revolutionary, by the end of the Han dynasty in AD 220 everybody accepted it not only as inevitable but indeed as proper. From this time historians have condemned any subsequent division of the country as shameful interludes between periods when the country was united under powerful ruling houses, preferably Chinese. The Han Empire was one of the most glorious of a series of empires which the Chinese created during the following two thousand years.

During the rebellion which brought about the end of the Ch'in house, the struggle for mastery of China finally reduced itself to that between two leaders, a nobleman of the old type named Hsiang Yü, who desired a return to the pre-Ch'in feudal organization of China, and a less colourful but more cunning peasant general, Liu Pang. After a war lasting five years, the peasant leader triumphed. The Han dynasty which he established lasted for four hundred years (206 BC–AD 220) with one short break in which an usurper was on the throne.

Liu Pang, or Emperor Kao-tsung as he became, professed to admire the feudal system which the First Emperor had destroyed, but in fact he governed through a system as authoritarian and centralized as that of his hated predecessor. However, he was much wiser than the First Emperor in enlisting the support of the scholars, particularly the Confucians. They faithfully served his purpose by extolling the virtues of an ideal but hypothetical early Chou régime under which they claimed that China was united under and obedient to a single ruler. Thus, to quote Fitzgerald,★ 'The First Emperor tried to destroy the memory of the past, the Han sovereigns, more subtle than he, succeeded in distorting it'. Confucianism became the pillar of state policy and the scholars developed into a new aristocracy of education which took the place of the old landed aristocracy. Throughout the following centuries they administered China with remarkable efficiency and patronized the arts on a scale unknown in any other great civilization.

The first Han Emperor rid himself of any possible embarrassment from his

China, London, 1935.

generals by degrading or destroying them. At the same time he created a façade of feudalism by making members of his family kings—but only of small and closely supervised territories. However, a later Emperor considered even this a source of possible danger and in 144 BC decreed that when a feudal lord died, his land should be divided between all his sons. Thus these feudal territories became more numerous but even smaller and more impotent.

In 141 BC Emperor Wu, 'The Martial Emperor', a man of restless ambition who was determined to govern absolutely, came to the throne. During the peaceful reign of his predecessor Emperor Wên (179–156 BC), China had recovered from the exhaustion of the Ch'in wars and the rebellions which established the Han. The country was sufficiently prosperous and strong to embark upon a series of campaigns which vastly increased the size of the Chinese Empire by bringing into it large areas of the south which had been independent. The Han armies were able to deal with the ever serious threat from the Hsiung-nu peoples in the north, and in a series of valiant campaigns they crossed Central Asia and reached almost to the borders of the Roman Empire. The Chinese paid dearly for the megalomania of Emperor Wu. Their records tell us that between 129 and 90 BC they lost over a quarter of a million of their best fighting men. The actual total may well have been double that.

One of the most stirring exploits of these years was a mission undertaken by the general Chang Ch'ien. In 165 BC a nomad tribe known in Chinese as the Ta Yüeh Chi were defeated by the Hsiung-nu and fled westwards. In 138 BC Emperor Wu sent Chang Ch'ien into Central Asia to find them and to try to enlist their support against the Hsiung-nu, hoping thereby to turn the nomads' western flank. The Hsiung-nu captured the Chinese general and kept him prisoner for ten years. He finally escaped and continued his search westwards. He reached the Ili Valley but discovered that the Ta Yüeh Chi had continued their migration farther west. He pressed on and passed through Ferghana, an area near Kokand in Russian Central Asia, only to learn that he would have to go still farther to the southwest. He finally caught up with them in Bactria, the most eastern end of Alexander's domain. By this time the Ta Yüeh Chi were so comfortably installed and with the prospects of rich lands to plunder lying before them in the south that, despite Chang Ch'ien's exhortations, they understably refused to go back to the Far East merely to serve the Han Emperor's purpose. The Chinese turned for home. En route the Hsiung-nu again captured Chang Ch'ien, but after only a year's further captivity he managed to escape again and make his way once more to China after an absence of twelve years in all.

Chang Ch'ien's report gave information of the lands he had crossed which included some of the most appalling that a traveller could encounter. It included a piece of information which greatly interested the Chinese Emperor. Reporting on the people of Ta Yüan or Ferghana he stated, 'They have grape-wine and many excellent horses. These are blood-sweating horses whose stock is the offspring of the Heavenly Horses'. The Chinese, it should be noted, are not like the steppe people born to the saddle. Their campaigns against the Hsiung-nu had forced them to adopt cavalry warfare and the Emperor was quick to see that finer horses would provide him with a major weapon against the expert horsemen of the north.

The Chinese during the 2nd century BC had steadily been extending their control out into Kansu province and thence into Central Asia itself. Chang Ch'ien's second expedition in 115 BC secured the route along which Chinese embassies seeking some of these superior horses were able to reach Ferghana. Hitherto the King of Ferghana had felt no reason to fear the distant Chinese and was not willing to part with the stock. One Chinese embassy was rash enough to try to carry off some by force. They paid for their lack of courtesy by being massacred. This was not the kind of treatment which Emperor Wu, by now thoroughly respected throughout the Far East, was willing to tolerate even in far-off Central Asia. In 104 BC he sent General Li Kuang-li with a motley army across the 2,000 miles separating the two countries to enforce his wishes. The journey through terrible and inhospitable areas bled the strength of this ill-prepared army. To feed it General Li was forced to capture every city he reached. Finally, at Ta Yüan he was defeated and forced to retreat to China. The Emperor, ignorant of the accomplishments of even this unsuccessful expedition, refused to allow Li Kuang-li to re-enter China and ordered him to remain encamped just outside the borders. Only the intervention of his sister, a favourite of the imperial harem, saved him from death, the usual fate of failed Han generals.

In 102 BC, the Emperor sent Li Kuang-li reinforcements of 60,000 men and ordered him to renew the campaign. This time, more experienced in long-distant warfare, the general reached the capital of Ta Yüan, besieged it and forced its inhabitants to sue for peace. The price he demanded for sparing the city and returning to China was some of the finest horses and 3,000 of inferior quality together with food for his starving army. From that time onwards Ta Yüan remained friendly to the Han Emperor. China was now for the first time a Central Asian power with outposts beyond the Pamirs. Chinese silk crossed Asia to adorn Roman ladies, who valued it for covering them in a manner which still made them look undressed.

Such strenuous and costly efforts to obtain horses emphasize the importance of the threat from the Hsiung-nu. The campaigns against them were many-sided. In order to turn their flank in the east, the Han invaded and settled part of North Korea. It was not until 51 B C that the threat from the Hsiung-nu was for a time halted. The horde at that time had split into two and the southern half paid homage to the Chinese Emperor.

Plates 22, 25, 29

Thus the first hundred and fifty years of the Han dynasty was a period of great expansion and of many new introductions. Chinese horizons expanded in all directions. A great deal of effort and history lies behind the sculptures of horses here illustrated which surrounded the tomb in Shensi of a general named Ho Ch'ü-ping. This man was the illegitimate son of the elder sister of a singing girl called Wei Ch'ing who, according to the records, had captivated the Emperor Wu by her glossy black hair and gleaming teeth. She was taken into the imperial harem in 139 BC. Ho Ch'ü-ping was victorious against the Hsiung-nu in 123 BC and was ennobled as a marquis. In 121 he took an expedition over 300 miles beyond Kanchou in modern Kansu. Among the many treasures he brought back was said to be an image in gold worshipped by the Hsiung-nu chief. Historians have speculated that this may have been the first image of the Buddha to enter China. Buddhism was at this time first making its way across Central Asia.

In 119 BC Ho Ch'ü-ping penetrated 1,600 miles into Central Asia bringing back with him ninety Hsiung-nu chieftains as prisoners. This active method of combatting the northern tribes proved more effective than the static defensive system based on the Great Wall. Chinese prestige throughout Central Asia and especially in the important Tarim basin area leading into China stood high and the Chinese Empire could relax for a few years from fear of the Hunnish tribes in the north.

It has not been ascertained for sure that the tomb in Shensi is indeed that of Ho Ch'ü-ping nor is the exact date of its erection certain. The general died in 117 BC, and most historians consider that the sculptures belong to approximately the same period. The problem has a certain interest in relation to the kind of horse represented, for at this time the Chinese first began to import from Central Asia types of horses superior to the small steppe horse which they and their enemies had used for centuries. Helen Fernald distinguishes three types of horses represented in Han art; the common steppe pony, the Ferghana 'heavenly' horses, and a third type which may have been the result of cross-breeding between the pony and the Ferghana horse. This the Chinese could have obtained and maintained in contacts with tribes like the Wu-sun living between China and Ferghana.* But it is difficult and dangerous to try to identify a breed from the work of artists or craftsmen. The best known of the sculptures is an almost life-sized figure of a horse standing over a fallen bearded

Helen E. Fernald: 'Chinese Art and the Wu-sun Horse', *Annual of the Royal Ontario Museum Division of Art and Archaeology*, 1959.

figure holding a bow in his left hand and plunging a spear into the side of the horse   *Plate 29*
with his right. The artist obviously intended to represent the figure of a fallen
northern 'barbarian' and considering the period and complete unfamiliarity of
Chinese artists with portraiture, he has succeeded remarkably well. The short legs,
heavy body and thick neck of the horse are undoubtedly those of a steppe breed.

From a stylistic point of view the whole group is of great interest. They are, of
course, the first monumental sculpture of China and as such are partly traditional
and partly experimental. The horse straddling the fallen barbarian looks back to the
bronze casting traditions of earlier centuries. Its closest parallel is a pair of small
bronze horses of 6th to 3rd centuries BC in the William Rockhill Nelson Gallery,
Kansas City. All the conventions for indicating anatomical features such as the
muscles on the legs and the shape of the head have been faithfully transformed into
stone. However, being unfamiliar with the material and technique, possibly introduced from the west, the artist has not dared to cut through the granite to produce
a figure which is completely independent of the rock from which it is shaped. It
thus gives the impression of two bas-reliefs placed together.

However, some of the other horses, especially the one which seems to be leaping
out of the rock from which it is carved, look ahead to the clay models of the more
thoroughbred type of horse which was beginning to enter China at this time. They
also indicate the new direction which the art was to follow. Prior to the Han
dynasty, the direction of Chinese art, as the bronzes show, was completely away
from naturalism; man and his surroundings hardly enter into his repertoire of art
motifs. The decoration of the bronzes was based on animal forms but they were so
highly stylized that it is often impossible to identify the animal intended. Towards
the end of the Chou period, from about the 6th century BC, more naturalistic
animals and even early figures of man appear in the bronzes, but only rarely.

With the Han dynasty, artists seem suddenly to have taken an absorbing interest
in everything they saw about them. Man and his world, from the landscape in
which he lived, his occupations and amusements down to the most humble domestic
utensil find manifold reflection. A striving for naturalism is the natural corollary
of this new interest in the world. With naturalism came that interest in depicting
movement which remained a preoccupation of Chinese art in all subsequent periods.

Thus the leaping horse looks ahead also to the bas-reliefs of later Han tombs on   *Plates 19, 21, 23*
which powerfully built horses gallop across battle scenes. The manner in which it
remains locked to the stone from which it springs is the result of the artist's inability
to match technique and idea, an extremely rare failing in Chinese art.

Seldom do we catch Chinese art in such a moment of indecision. For just this reason the horses, looking like half-finished works in a sculptor's studio faithfully reflect the atmosphere of early Han art. They are experimental and tentative, alive with new ideas and techniques and above all robust and energetic.

Two of the original six are in the University Museum, Philadelphia.

What a distance lies between the heavy repetitive low reliefs of horses from Han times and the high reliefs of similar subjects from the tomb of Emperor T'ai Tsung*, founder of the T'ang dynasty! They were commissioned in AD 637, and, according to tradition, are based on original designs by Yen Li-pen, one of the outstanding painters of the day. The approach is basically the same as that of the Han reliefs, but the T'ang figures breathe the full and naturalistic spirit of T'ang sculpture which we shall see in the Buddhist works of the period. Each horse has its marked personality, in keeping with the love and lore of horses so characteristic of the Chinese, and this particular relief has the vitality and movement which we associate with Chinese painting. It is, perhaps, not so stirring as the contemporary tomb figures discussed in Chapter VII which can be taken as the continuation of the naturalistic tendency in lay sculpture. It is interesting to trace the developing mastery of naturalistic representation outside Buddhist sculpture, the development of what the Chinese call the 'life-breath' in works starting from the Han dynasty, through the Northern Wei 6th century AD examples, to the early and the full T'ang achievements. The terracotta figures of valiant steeds representing the full flowering of this development are surely among the world's masterpieces of animal sculpture.

Plate 109

We know little about the horses round Ho Ch'ü-ping's tomb. The other huge boulders are even more difficult to understand or place within the general context of Chinese art. They are simply large pieces of worn stone, the surfaces of which anonymous craftsmen have briefly modelled to represent a buffalo-like creature eating a small animal and a gigantic demon hugging and biting a small bear. These figures lie so completely outside the known traditions of Chinese art that one is tempted to think that they might have been brought back by General Ho Ch'ü-ping as trophies from his campaigns. Animals in conflict are often found in the bronze horse trappings of the nomads though no monumental examples of this kind have appeared. The bear is a cult animal of the steppe people, but it also found its way into Chinese art of the Han dynasty. The demon eating a bear may be a Chinese satire on the habits of the barbarians of the steppes but the animal figure in the background carries no such overtones. Lack of comparative material forces us to keep a completely open mind on these impressive but perplexing boulders.

Plate 26

Notes on the plates on page 73

19

21

20

22

25

26

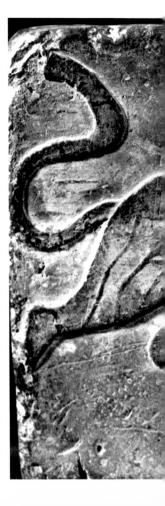

27

28

29

NOTES ON THE PLATES TO CHAPTER II

18 PART OF THE GREAT WALL north of Peking.

19 A HORSE AND GROOM—detail from a rubbing of a stone relief in a tomb in Chiating, Szechwan province. Height 49 cm (19 1/2″).

20 HEAD OF A POTTERY TOMB FIGURE of a horse. *Musée Cernuschi, Paris.*

21 HORSES AND CHARIOTS—detail from a rubbing of a stone relief in one of the Wu Liang tombs, Shantung province.

22 ONE OF THE STONE HORSES from the tomb of General Ho Ch'ü-ping, Shensi province, who died in 117 BC. See *p. 62.*

23 A HAN TOMB GUARDIAN—rubbing from a stone relief in a tomb in Chêng-tu, Szechwan province.

24 PART OF THE GREAT WALL north of Peking.

25 A STONE HORSE from the tomb of General Ho Ch'ü-ping. See *p. 62.*

26 BOULDER CARVED as a demon devouring a small bear. See *p. 64.*

27/8 HUNTING AND WILD ANIMAL SCENES—details from baked clay funerary ware. *Musée Guimet, Paris.*

29 STONE STATUE OF A HORSE of the steppes breed standing over a wounded barbarian, tomb of General Ho Ch'ü-ping. See *pp. 62/63.*

III YÜN-KANG

IN AD 460 a Buddhist monk named T'an-yao became Administrator of Monks under the Northern Wei dynasty. This relatively unimportant administrative appointment was to result in one of the world's most impressive artistic testimonies to religious faith. Behind it lay two and a half centuries of political confusion and religious effort which we must here briefly outline before the cave temples of Yün-kang can be appreciated.

The Han dynasty collapsed at the beginning of the 3rd century AD. Its four centuries created a nation and forged an empire. In so doing it set a pattern for the following two thousand years of Chinese civilization. The downfall of the dynasty was due to a number of causes. Intrigues at court progressively undermined the authority of the Han emperors. Place-seeking by ambitious families of empresses was partly responsible, but, more seriously, a body of eunuchs, originally created to guard the imperial harem, did most to undermine the prestige of the ruling house. These men of low rank and little education gradually assumed wide powers outside their original function. They were in a position to influence the Emperor, and, especially if he was a minor, to keep him in ignorance of practical affairs and of true conditions throughout the vast kingdom. They filled important offices with their favourites, and servants of the Emperor found that loyalty to the throne and to a code of just administration, the basis of Confucian teaching, was extremely difficult. The eunuchs only granted positions to their creatures in return for heavy bribes. This forced the recipients of these positions to recoup themselves by heavy exactions on those they governed with the result that economic distress was widespread. The eunuchs hid this from the Emperor and interpreted any suggestion by a loyal administrator of the need for reform as proof of seditious intentions. Thus they speedily disposed of any general or servant courageous or unwise enough to resent their evil influence. In this period there first appeared the secret societies pressing for reform which from time to time have distinguished Chinese politics down to the 19th century. During the second half of the 2nd century AD the scholar-officials banded together to try to enforce reform, but the eunuchs outwitted them. The large armies which the Emperor had recruited to suppress the numerous popular risings then seized the opportunity to destroy the eunuchs. The Han administrative machinery collapsed and the Empire rapidly fell into anarchy. In the disturbances following the fall of the dynasty, the capital was sacked and the palace looted. The country was split up into a number of rival kingdoms and the north left defenceless before the nomads who were waiting their opportunity. During the following centuries many Chinese fled to the south bringing the civilization of the north to the Yangtze valley which from that time became an increasingly important cultural centre. While north China was having its 'dark ages' the south, to a degree, preserved traditional Chinese ways. It gained an important victory against the nomads at Fei-shui in AD 387 after which the invaders were content to leave the south, topographically unsuited to their mobile type of warfare, in comparative peace.

The cultural history of north China would have been barren indeed had it not been for the nomad tribe which established what became known as the Northern Wei dynasty (386–532). The T'o-pa clan who founded it were a branch of the Hsien-pei nomads who until then had lived by raising cattle in the upper valleys of the Shara-muren. They were a mixture of Mongol and Tungusic strains, with probably more Mongol blood than any other. Until they settled in China their contacts with the Chinese people, as was usual with these nomad peoples, had taken the form of plundering raids on the more prosperous settled frontier lands. In the 1st century AD their enemies the Hsiung-nu moved westwards and the Hsien-pei expanded into the Gobi plateau. Like many successful nomad conquerors they owed much to tribal heroes who reorganized their forces. T'an Shih-huai in the 2nd century and K'o Pi-nêng in the 3rd century united the Hsien-pei. Their enmity to the Hsiung-nu brought them political contacts with the Chin dynasty, one of the numerous Chinese dynasties that rose and fell in this chaotic period, which succeeded in forming an alliance with them against the Hsiung-nu. They remained nomads until about AD 393 when they defeated the later Yen dynasty in north China. Soon after this their King began to call himself King of Wei to indicate that he considered himself the legal successor of the Han, and thus openly challenged the right of the Eastern Chin dynasty in the south to consider itself the inheritor of the Han state and Han culture.

Once established within the Great Wall, the T'o-pa rapidly found themselves forced to administer their newly conquered territories through the Chinese system by creating a hierarchy of feudal lords, generals and governors. It was natural that they should rely upon the resident and experienced Chinese to provide the civil administration while at first they kept the military power in nomad hands. However, the T'o-pa, unlike some later nomad invaders, seem to have been comparatively liberal in outlook towards the Chinese population they controlled. They early recognized the superiority of Chinese cultural standards as established in the Han Empire and encouraged their re-establishment. The Chinese farmers, in their turn, weary of unsettled conditions, were quick to appreciate that their best chance of survival lay in the settled rule of the T'o-pa, and they willingly co-operated with the invaders. From about 435 onwards when peace was secure the integration of Chinese and nomads proceeded rapidly. Chinese were allowed to enter the army and nomads married Chinese women. From about 462 an aristocracy began to form regardless of nomad or Chinese origin. The Chinese farmers prospered while those nomads who preferred their traditional way of life grew impoverished. Finally the Chinese system completely ousted that of the nomads. It was even laid down by law that the population should wear Chinese instead of nomad dress—a change that is reflected in the dress styles of the statues at Yün-kang. Similarly the sculptural styles of Yün-kang show a steady reversion to the traditions of Chinese art.

Without doubt the most important event during these chaotic centuries was the rapid spread of the Buddhist faith. It entered China in the 1st century AD and seems even then to have gained a small following among the court and nobility. By the 2nd century AD zealous Buddhist missionaries from India were beginning to make the long journey to China, and the translation of Buddhist *sūtras* began to be an important aspect of religious life. However, in these early centuries the Chinese had only the vaguest ideas of this foreign faith, and they paid the same honours to the Buddha as they did to native Chinese deities such as Huang-ti, the Yellow Emperor, and Lao-tzu, the founder of Taoism. It seems that the first temple dedicated to Buddhism was built at the end of the 2nd century. This was probably a *stūpa* containing a gilt-bronze statue of the Buddha. The faith seems to have made steady, if not spectacular progress, and by the beginning of the 4th century the northern areas contained no less than 893 temples dedicated to the Buddha. The excavation of cave-temples at the great Buddhist site of Tun-huang which leads into the deserts of Central Asia began in the mid-4th century (see Chapter V).

By the time the T'o-pa appeared in north China, Buddhism was firmly established in that part of the country. The religion was over eight hundred years old in India and had developed in its *mahāyāna* or 'Greater Vehicle' form a system with a whole hierarchy of divinities and an impressive ritual, appealing to simple people. The mahāyānists taught that salvation, or escape from the endless painful circle of birth–death–rebirth could be achieved by everybody and not, as *hinayānists*, the followers of the 'Lesser Vehicle', claimed, only by the few who could follow the life of an ascetic monk. One of the distinguishing features of mahāyāna Buddhism was the concept of the *bodhisattva*, a being who, through a series of good lives, had earned the right to Buddhahood and complete extinction, but, to help suffering humanity towards the same goal, elects to delay the final consummation. This concept produced a whole pantheon of popular divinities and what was in fact almost a new religion. Mahāyānists looked on Sākyamuni, the founder of Buddhism, as only one of a series of countless Buddhas of infinite worlds of the past and future. Maitreya, the Buddha of the Future, who would come to lead suffering humanity to bliss in his heaven, became even more popular in China in the 5th and 6th centuries than was Sākyamuni. The native religions and ethical systems seemed colourless compared with the mahāyāna system, with its rituals and its promise of blissful heavens for the virtuous. At the same time the Buddhist scriptures were translated into good Chinese providing intellectuals with arguments against their adversaries trained for centuries in literary ways. Buddhism became by far the most popular religion, but by its very nature lived in peace with native beliefs.

Originally the T'o-pa clan had no knowledge of Buddhism, but for a foreign invader Buddhism had obvious practical benefits for it preached humility and peacefulness. Hence a population devoted to Buddhism would be easy to govern. On the other hand, nomad kings saw no disadvantage in honouring a religion which promised rewards for goodness and for the observance of its message. It is important to appreciate that the native Chinese gods meant little to the invaders. On the contrary, they were even suspect. One northern ruler defended his support of Buddhism by saying, 'We were born out of the marches . . . Buddha being a barbarian god is the one we should worship'. They suspected Confucians as being loyal to the Chinese emperor and this forced them to seek their educated men and administrators among the ranks of the Buddhists and Taoists. However, the Taoists were naturally jealous of the success of Buddhism, and this combined with other causes to check the progress of the faith. In times of distress monasteries and convents offered an attractive means of escape from the troubled world, but too large a class of unproductive monks and nuns, together with the land they controlled, created a social and economic problem. The anti-Buddhist measures were occasionally severe, but never reached the proportions of Western religious persecutions.

Soon after AD 439 Emperor T'ai-wu of the Northern Wei dynasty became converted to Taoism, and in 445 he initiated a persecution of Buddhism. This was the first of four main persecutions which the faith suffered in China during the following centuries. Fortunately in this instance many monks and nuns were able to find sanctuary in the south which welcomed them. T'ai-wu died in 452 and his successor immediately relaxed the rigid laws. Henceforth the civil and religious interests seem to have been reconciled on terms of mutual respect and appreciation. By about AD 500, Buddhism was by far the most powerful religious force throughout the whole of the north and south of China.

The spread of the Buddhist faith owed much to the courage of Indian missionaries who crossed Central Asia to teach the Chinese, and of Chinese pilgrims who went to India to visit the holy sites and to study at the universities, and then returned to their native country to spread the faith. By the end of the 2nd century AD such visits became more frequent with the increasing popularity of Buddhism. The majority travelled through Central Asia, but some attempted the sea route from Tonkin via Java, Sumatra and the Malay peninsular to India, and a few travelled the even more dangerous routes from Kunming along the valleys of the Chindwin and the Irrawaddy or through Tibet and Nepal. Each route had its own difficulties, and the hazards were enough to daunt all but the most zealous and intrepid.

Those who attempted the Central Asian route generally left China through Tun-huang (see Chapter V), travelling some 300 miles into the desert, where they were faced with a choice between a northern and a southern route round the wastelands of the Tarim basin. The northern route passed through the oases of Karashar and Kucha to Kashgar, the southern through those of Miya, Keriya, Khotan, Yarkand and made its way down into India. The distances they travelled varied from between 6,000 to 10,000 miles. The routes they took were, of course, well known, for they were some of the old silk routes along which the much sought after Chinese product had since Han times passed, finally to reach the Mediterranean. Along them travelled also the nomadic peoples. In unsettled times the attacks of these tribes added to the pilgrims' hardships. At the various oases Buddhism acted as a binding and civilizing force on the semi-barbarous peoples and later Western explorers such as Sir Aural Stein, le Coq and Otani discovered in these bleak wastelands the remains of great works of devotional art, now often eroded and buried under the sands.

It is estimated that between the 3rd and 8th centuries two hundred Chinese attempted the journey, but that only forty-two reached India, completed their studies and returned safely to their homes. One of the most famous was Fa-hsien who left China for India in 399, crossed Central Asia, travelled through India down to Ceylon—crossed to Java and finally reached home by sea after a journey lasting fifteen years in all.

The task of translating the Buddhist scriptures into Chinese occupied the lives of many of the earliest Indian missionaries to China. Dharmarakṣa went to China in 284 where he spent thirty years translating some 211 texts. The most famous monk translator, Kumārajīva, who founded a great translating workshop, was in China from 383 to 413. As the texts were translated, so the distinctions between the various schools of Buddhist thought became known to the Chinese. However, broadly speaking, few Chinese were attracted to the finer and more obscure teachings which have always appealed to the subtle Indian mind.

The Chinese seized on the more dramatic episodes in the life of the Teacher such as Western artists did in depicting moments in the life of Christ. For instance, frequently in Yün-kang one finds niches with two Buddhas seated side by side. This is a representation inspired by the *Saddharma Puṇḍarīka Sūtra* or the 'Lotus of the True Law', generally known as the *Lotus Sūtra*. This scripture was written in approximately the 1st century AD and was translated into Chinese five times before AD 406, the most authentic version being that of the monk translator Kumārajīva. It rapidly became one of the most important texts in the East. The sūtra is written in a dramatic form which grips the reader while at the same time instructing him. It demands of the believer a simple faith in its teachings and makes of the Buddha a god rather than a human being who has attained enlightenment. Its teachings have been summarized as follows: 'The Buddha is divine. Through faith in his word all living creatures can be saved, not merely for an unknowable nirvāṇa but for an existence in the paradises of the Buddha. In his faith the true believer shall be aided by the words of the sūtra and the active presence of the great bodhisattvas.'*

J. L. Davidson: *The Lotus Sūtra in Chinese Art*. Yale, 1954, p. 4.

One of the most dramatic episodes in the long sūtra occurs when a stūpa suddenly appears in the sky containing the relics of the extinct Prabhūtaratna Buddha. Myriads of Buddhas from all the universe appear. In a scene of great brilliance, Śākyamuni rises into the sky, opens the stūpa using his finger as a key, thereby revealing the extinct Buddha who says: 'Excellent, excellent, Lord Śākyamuni.' The two Buddhas then sit together in the stūpa and discuss the faith. This was a popular theme for religious sculptors and symbolized the teaching of the Lotus Sūtra.

In general the Chinese simplified, synthesized and expended their tremendous energies less in philosophical disputation than in creating, as at Yün-kang, vast artistic monuments to a sincere and simply comprehended faith.

During the period immediately following the fall of the Han when Chinese influence waned, the scattered peoples in Central Asia became culturally orientated towards India. We have seen how the Hsuing-nu drove the Yüeh-chi out of their homeland in north China. They finally settled in northwest India and established what became known as the Kushan dynasty. Its most powerful ruler was the Buddhist King Kanishka who probably came to the throne in AD 144. The Kushans established comparative peace throughout Central Asia, traded with China, Asia Minor, Egypt, Greece and Rome and took cultural influences from them all. At the beginning of the 3rd century Persia came under the Sassanian dynasty. Its art reverted to national traditions and strong influences from it reached into Central Asia and into north India.

The main area for the export of images was north-west India in the area of the old province of Gandhāra which occupies an area on the west bank of the Indus river comprising the Peshawar valley and the modern Swat, Buner and Bajaur.

Plates 146, 150 Here in the first centuries AD grew up an art which was a very complicated mixture of provincial Roman styles and Indian iconography. To the south lay the older,

Plates 155, 156 purely Indian, art centre of Mathurā. Between them they originated the Buddha and bodhisattva types which spread from India throughout the Far East as far as Japan. The influence in Gandhāra must at first have been mainly western, for the faces of the statues are Apollonian and their dress directly inspired by Roman toga styles. By the 3rd century, stucco, a technique of Iranian origin, augmented the grey schist of the earlier Gandhāran statues and this style continued into the 7th century when the area was devastated by the white Huns. This technique gave the sculptors far greater freedom of expression, and when Indian workmen began to replace the westerners, the figures became less humanistic in concept, softer and more supple, in conformity with Indian traditions. The dress changed from the toga styles to thinner draperies indicated by a series of ridges or strings over a body which is visible beneath them. The two styles seem to have co-existed in Gandhāra.

Afghanistan, the home of Gandhāran sculpture, was at this time a melting pot for influences from India, Iran and from classical sources. It was also the gateway into the desolate areas of Central Asia. Here is found the great Buddhist site of

Plates 142, 143 Bāmiyān which made a tremendous impact on Chinese travellers as they entered India. At Bāmiyān monasteries and temples carved from the sandstone cliff occupy more than a mile of the cliff face. Before the site was devastated by Genghis Khan it must have been a breathtaking example of devotional art and architecture. Two huge niches must have particularly impressed the Buddhist travellers, for they each house a colossal Buddha image, one 127 feet and the other over 167 feet high. One has draperies of typical Gandhāran style while the other has draperies modelled over cords which attach them to the body. They were probably made between the 3rd and 5th centuries. They served as the direct models for the colossi at Yün-kang and throughout the Far East. They contain, especially in the paintings behind and around them, not only Gandhāran and Indian influences but also strong echoes of Iranian art. The artistic give-and-take, the diverse influences working on the provincial arts of these areas, are extremely difficult to disentangle, especially since so much has been destroyed or buried beneath the sands.

Plates 30, 33

Before tracing the progress of this art along the famous 'Silk Route' one might well wonder what led Indians to create their temples inside the living rock and why they produced such huge statues to their gods. Cave temples are, of course, found in many religious systems throughout the world, but India, with its twelve hundred man-made caves, developed the idea more than any other people. Practical considerations naturally influenced the artists. They sought escape from the hostile, burning heat of the Indian sun and as K. J. Kandalawa pointed out, they were generally near trade routes and so situated as to afford seclusion and at the same time easy access to those passing along them.* Again it has been pointed out that Indian craftsmen by nature prefer sculpture to architecture. Their buildings thus tend to be sculptural *tours de force*. It was also, in view of their requirements, easier for the monks than to quarry and dress material. But, to look more deeply into this phenomenon, one finds that Indian ways of thought encourage man to seek God within himself. The darkness or semi-darkness of caves helps him to free himself from distracting external influences. The darkness the worshipper creates for himself in a cave leads to a loss of self, to a freedom from illusion and it helps him to find oneness with the divine. This darkness has also a positive function, for although it can be frightening, one must remember that the Indian wishes to see the terrifying as well as the benign aspects of his divinity. Again darkness is associated with death and Indian religions teach man to regard death as the essential preliminary to life.* The sites of these cave temples are also symbolic. For the Indian the mountain was not only identified with his god but was a symbol of eternity. In carving his temple into the rock he was approaching as near to his god and to eternity as he could. Nothing could come closer to his idea of the durability of the divine than the massive cliffs which he hollowed out.

K. J. Kandalawa, in *Lolit Kata,* No. 6, Oct. 1959.

M. Neff: 'The Origins of the Indian Cave Temple' in *Oriental Art*, vol. IV, No. 1, 1958, pp. 23-7.

Secondly one might ask why they created such giant sculptures. The huge statues attracted attention and commanded respect. They had to be huge to match their setting. Iconographically, they were intended to portray the superhuman qualities of the Buddha as described in the scriptures. Sākyamuni is portrayed in these colossi as Lord of the Universe.

Anybody unfamiliar with Buddhist devotional art may on first acquaintance be surprised by the seeming multiplication of identical images. The rows of identical images, the so-called 'Thousand Buddhas' which fill whole walls of these caves, also have a sanction in the Buddhist scriptures. Buddhist cosmology reckons time and space in terms of *kalpas*. A kalpa is an almost immeasurable length of time during which a world system comes into being and is destroyed. Buddhists define a kalpa by a fanciful simile. Suppose that there was a mountain of very hard rock and that a man wearing a robe of the finest cloth brushed it once every hundred years. The time taken for the cloth to wear away the mountain would be a kalpa. According to them we live in only one of many kalpas stretching into the past and into the future. Each kalpa has its hundreds of beings who have reached enlightenment and become Buddhas. The Thousand Buddhas are generally intended to represent the Buddhas of this kalpa of whom the last was Sākyamuni. However, sometimes the Thousand Buddhas represent manifestations of Sākyamuni—especially when they surround a niche containing two Buddhas, one of whom is Sākyamuni and the other Prabhūtaratna. Sometimes the artist carved a group of Seven Buddhas which include the last three Buddhas of the previous kalpa. A reading of any of the great Buddhist scriptures impresses the reader with the bewildering multiplicity of Buddhas and their manifestations in time and space. The Chinese sculptors did not intend to keep to the letter of the law—indeed they probably did not understand it very well—rather they aimed at awing the spectator by the immensity of the Buddhist world and at impressing him with his own insignificant position in time and place. At Yün-kang they succeeded admirably.

The official records of the Northern Wei dynasty, the *Wei-shu,* record that T'an-yao petitioned the Emperor that five caves should be excavated in the stone wall hewn out of the mountain ridge of the Wu-chou fortress near the capital, with one Buddhist statue carved in each cave. The tallest was 70 *chih* (54 ft.) and the others 60 *chih* (46 ft. 4 in.) high. The carvings were of exceptional excellence and unparalleled throughout the world. The actual date is not recorded but the event must have taken place in about AD 460 soon after the monk was appointed to his high position. It seems certain that the five statues of the Buddha were made for the benefit of the reigning Emperor and his four predecessors.

The Northern Wei conquered the state of Pei-liang in AD 439. This was an area in which Buddhism flourished and the monks and their equipment were moved to the Northern Wei capital, P'ing-ch'eng. This forced migration which probably included T'an Yao must have greatly increased religious activity at the capital. The priest survived the persecution of Buddhism with unshaken faith, lived to gain the complete confidence of the Emperor and to undertake the huge project at Yün-kang. To this he devoted the majority of his life. He probably died in the mid-480's aged between 70 and 80 years.

The styles of the sculptures at Yün-kang fall into two broad categories—the earlier works like the colossal figures which were created in fairly close accordance with imported models and perhaps even under the supervision of Central Asian workmen, and the later types which were far more Chinese in concept, feeling and execution. The origins of the first are by far the most difficult to trace. In addition to Mathurā, the far more native school, which influenced Gandhāran workmanship and which exported thousands of small devotional figures such as pilgrims could have carried back, the oases in Central Asia all had their own art which combined the styles of Gandhāra and Mathurā and added strong influences from Iran. The pilgrims would carry back either the small statues, approximately 6 inches high, or what is more probable, drawings of divinities. It was probably on these that the sculptors at Yün-kang based their huge works. The effort, imagination and zeal which led a people with little experience in sculpture, and none in large works of this nature, to undertake such a project is almost incredible.

Plate 33

Plates 36, 37, 153

The site in Central Asia which may have influenced the Yün-kang workmen most was at Kyzil near Kucha on the northern route round the desert to India. The caves found there are the most numerous and must have been the best known. Many pilgrims in search of Buddhist knowledge never went further than some of the Central Asian centres and many of the workmen from these oases travelled to China. At Kyzil about 170 caves were carved in the cliff overlooking the Muzart river. The figures are of stucco and the walls covered with clay prior to painting, but a number of the ceilings resemble those at Yün-kang. Unfortunately their dates have not been ascertained. However, they do not compare with those of Yün-kang in size, complexity of decoration or artistic skill.

Plate 144

Plate 33 shows Caves XX to XXVI at Yün-kang, that is to say seven of a total of about 42 caves. The group is dominated by Cave XX on the right containing a huge seated Buddha figure, the second largest of the site. Beyond the picture to the right are the other caves built under the inspiration of T'an-yao. Originally the huge figure was not exposed but concealed behind a front wall, traces of which can be

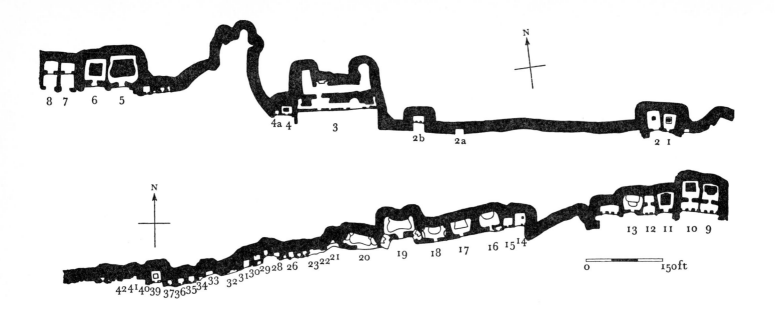

4 *Plan of the Yün-kang group, Shansi province. Top: Caves I to VIII. Bottom: Caves IX to XLII.*

seen in rows of Thousand Buddha niches at the right of the main figure. These small niches probably covered the whole of the outer wall. The carving of this huge cave into faulty strata of rock, as can be seen by the cracks across the figures, so weakened the cliff face that sometime before the Liao dynasty (12th century) the front wall collapsed covering the knees of the colossus and the legs of its attendants as well as the fore court with fallen rock both carved and uncarved. The area was excavated and cleared by the Japanese in 1940 leaving the cave in its present state.

The main figure is 44 feet high and seated in the *dhyāna,* or meditating position. On each side of the main Buddha is an attendant bodhisattva standing on a shallow lotus base, but these have almost entirely disappeared. The large figure on the left of the central figure is another Buddha 31 ft. 6 in. in height in a standing position. Above this figure are more niches containing Buddhas either singly or in pairs. One of these formed part of a row of niches on the front wall just below the ceiling when the cave was complete. At the top can be seen a celestial flying towards the main figure. The upper half of the main figure together with the carvings of halo and nimbus of the back wall is remarkably well preserved. The figures on the nimbus represent the Seven Buddhas of the Past, the last of which was Sākyamuni. The holes cut into the back wall probably held the ends of beams which supported a wooden building erected to protect what remained of the cave after the fall of the cliff face.

Plate 30

The proportions of the figure are exaggerated, with broad shoulders in conformity with the canonical descriptions of the Buddha's body. According to Buddhist belief his human body only concealed his true stature which could only be seen with the eye of faith. It had thirty-two attributes, marks of superhumanity. It was 18 feet tall, the shoulders 'curved' and the torso like a lion. The body in circumference was like a stately fig tree. 'Between the Lord's eyebrows was a woolly curl (ūrnā), soft like cotton and similar to a jasmine flower, to the moon, to a conch shell, to the filament of a lotus, to cow's milk, to a hoar frost's blossom.' Many-coloured light radiates from this hair tuft. This is clearly marked on the huge figures. The protuberance on the head, the usnīsa, was originally a turban and takes many forms in Buddha images. The nimbus signified divinity and sanctity and the flames on the halo denote the fiery energy which radiates from the bodies of great men—a power increased by meditation.* The eyes in the main figure are most gracefully proportioned and what is unusual, shown wide open. The black pupils to the eyes are not original, but were large black-glazed cones inserted at a later date. The clean-cut lines of the contours and the simplicity of carving give the figure great strength and calmness. The manner of representing the folds is like cords attached to the body alternating with incised lines. The zig-zag lines on the robes are reminiscent of native Indian sculpture.

Such huge figures naturally dominate the Yün-kang façade. They are eloquent expressions of a simple faith in which the aim is to portray the Buddha as a benign, supernatural divinity, calm and dignified amidst the bustle of the world. This is the early Yün-kang style in which a certain naturalism inherited from Gandhāran work and its echoes in Central Asia persists. The sculptors were too absorbed in the vastness of their project to create the new styles and impose the Chinese traditions as they did in the caves carved after the Five Caves of T'an-yao. They are more concerned with iconographical accuracy and with expressing volume than with the more traditional linear energy.

Plates 31, 32 and 38 are taken from Cave XVIII, which together with Cave XIX was probably the first of the caves worked by T'an-yao. Its workmanship, apart from a few niches added later, is uniformly of the earliest period of activity at Yün-kang. The main image of the cave is a huge figure of Sākyamuni. *Plates 32 and 38* show the left attendant bodhisattva of the main figure. It stands between the main Buddha and its attendant Buddha. Above and around the head are five figures, two in full length and three half bodies. These are five of the ten *arhats* or disciples of Sākyamuni Buddha. The other five are on the opposite wall. Together they enable us to

5 *Study of the drapery folds on the Buddhas in Cave XIX, Yün-kang.*

* E. Conze: *Buddhism.* Oxford, 1951, pp. 36–38.

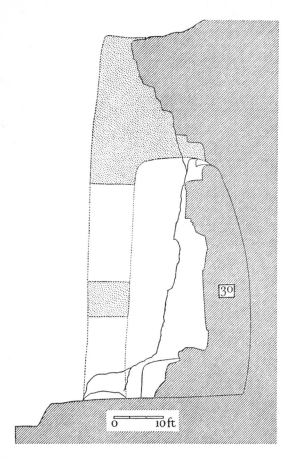

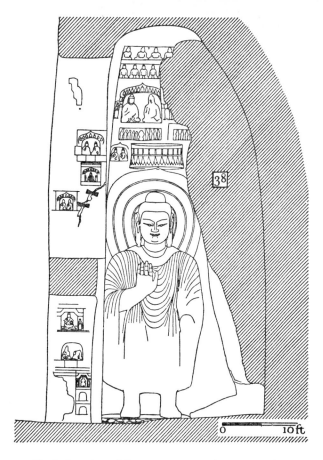

6 *Vertical section of Cave XX, Yün-kang. See the same seated Buddha on plate 30.*

7 *Vertical section of Cave XVIII, Yün-kang. See plate 38.*

identify the main Buddha as Sākyamuni. It is possible to identify the two full length figures more precisely as Ananda and Māhā-Kāśyapa. These figures are unique in the whole of Yün-kang and indeed seem to have been a Chinese invention. Unlike the majority of the sculptures of this site they have a marked individuality of feature and a personality which makes them stand out from all the works of the caves. The Chinese have no great gifts for depicting personality in sculpture; it was left to the Japanese to develop this aspect of sculpture with notable success. The head of the bodhisattva is adorned with an ornate crown modelled on prototypes developed in Central Asia. A small figure of a meditating Buddha is seated in the central disc. Tassels hang from the other discs to suggest that the crown was attached to the hair by a large pin.

Plate 31 shows the attendant Buddha on the west wall of which the head alone is over 6 feet high. A closely clinging monastic robe covers the body. This was originally painted red, the face white and the hair black. A green moustache and

86

8   *Frontal diagram of Cave XVIII, Yün-kang, showing the distribution of major and minor figures around the central standing Buddha. See plates 31 and 32.*

beard are also represented. The black eye-pupils were inserted at a later date. The right hand held at the breast has webbed fingers which are one of the thirty-two superior marks. The now destroyed left hand probably once held the end of the robe. Scholars who have studied at the site consider that this huge head with its complicated and powerfully carved halo is one of the most impressive works in the whole of Yün-kang.

Plates 34 and 35 show how rapidly the Chinese tradition began to reassert itself over the styles imported into China from Central Asia and even further west. They are of two striking details from the reveals of the entrance arches leading from the anterooms to the main rooms of Caves VII and VIII carved *c*. 465–470. The anteroom of Cave VII has now almost completely disappeared but that of Cave VIII is better preserved. In these two caves a remarkable harmony was established between the native and the imported styles. The heavy rounded bodies recall the giant Buddha of Cave XX, but the method of indicating draperies and jewellery by tense incised   *Plate 30* lines is typical of Chinese art of the Han dynasty onwards. The flying angel has all the sense of movement and vitality which are the essence of Chinese art. Here the Chinese workmen felt free from the need for keeping to foreign models. The divinities themselves with their many heads and arms are of Indian origin and originally were not even Buddhist. They represent the Hindu Vishnu, one of the trinity comprising Brahmā, Vishnu and Siva. This is a benign divinity, 'the preserver', and one of India's oldest gods, older by far than Buddhism. But Buddhism wherever it went was able peacefully to absorb the divinities of other religions into itself. The usual attributes shown in the various arms of Vishnu are the mace, the lotus, the conch shell and the wheel. Here the top pair of arms hold discs representing the sun and the moon. The middle left hand holds a bow and probably the middle right hand held an arrow though this has now disappeared. The lower left hand holds a small phoenix. The figure is seated on a phoenix which holds a large pearl in its beak and has scale-like plumage. The iconography of the figure is completely mixed. Vishnu's usual vehicle is *garuda,* a kind of eagle and the enemy of serpents, while the phoenix is a traditional Chinese motif.

The figure from Cave VII has only three heads and four arms, the two subsidiary heads differing in expression and headdress from that of the centre. It has no phoenix on which to ride and instead of locks of hair, an ornate crown. To the right of the figure is a storeyed pillar like a pagoda, the storeys decorated with a chevron pattern. Sometimes in these pillars children support the storeys. Here they have been preserved but freed from the supporting function. At the top is a spray of lotus or acanthus leaves from which emerges an *aupapāduka* with hands reverently pressed together. In the sūtra entitled *Amitāyus-Dhyāna-Sūtra* or 'Meditation on Buddha Amitāyus' translated twelve times into Chinese from 148 onwards, the faithful are instructed by dogma to meditate in such a way that they will be reborn in the paradise of the Buddha Amitābha. When a being who fully understands the truth of the sūtras is about to die, Amitāyus with his attendant bodhisattvas and retinue will bring a seat of purple gold and approach him with words of praise, saying, 'O my son in the Law! thou hast practised the Mahāyāna doctrine; thou hast understood and believed the highest truth; therefore I now come to meet and welcome thee'. He and the thousand created Buddhas offer hands at once. When that man looks at his own body, he will find himself seated on that purple gold seat; he will then, stretching forth his folded hands, praise and eulogize all the Buddhas. As quick as thought he will be born in the lake of seven jewels, of that country. The purple gold seat on which he sits is like a magnificent jewel-flower, and will open after a night;

the new-comer's body becomes purple gold in colour, and he will also find under his feet a seven-jewelled lotus-flower. Even in this representation it will be seen that the sculptor has given the lotus-flower seven petals to represent the seven jewels. The sūtra goes through the means of salvation for various classes, and according to its teaching everybody, on salvation, is reborn into the pure land on a lotus. For even the most wicked, salvation is possible if they utter the name Buddha Amitāyas with sincerity. Such a type of Buddhism captured the minds of simple people from China to Japan and displaced the profound teachings of more obscure scriptures.

The creatures of the early style made their appeal to the spirit rather than to the senses. It was intended to express an ideal dignity rather than an ideal beauty; too much realism would have detracted the worshipper and destroyed its appeal. Disinterest in the human body, the prison of the spirit, is a Buddhist tenet. The Chinese had no interest in physical proportions and no tradition for depicting them. Even more, they felt a discomfort in dealing with the unclothed figure. Unlike the Indians, the Chinese consider nudity not only uninteresting but also unnatural, especially in their own climate. Behind the massive nobility and the dignity of early Yün-kang is simply a sincere attempt to idealize a deep religious experience.

The style following the first phase at Yün-kang can be seen in Cave XV a. It is a *Plates 36, 37* reinterpretation of all the influences that reached China—Hellenistic, Gandhāran, Indian, Iranian and Central Asian—in Chinese terms. The speed with which this was done indicates the strength of the tradition behind it. The sculptors were now more concerned with making a direct appeal to the senses through beauty of line and softness of expression. As Sickman says, 'The linear, geometric style, inherent in Han art, soon began to modify the forms, reducing still more any naturalism that *L. Sickman: The Art and* Central Asia had retained from the modified Hellenism of Gandhāra and the sen- *Architecture of China.* London, suousness of Indian sculpture'.* Stylization decreased the naturalism of the earlier *1956.* figures and their heavy esoteric dignity. The colossi disappear in favour of smaller figures more lovingly carved. The bodies are swathed in voluminous robes which completely hide the body and emphasize planes rather than volumes. Rhythmically arranged skirts drape symmetrically over the bases. Movement re-enters Chinese sculpture not only in the smaller flying angels but in the main figures and their attendants who sway gracefully to give meaning to the swirl of the drapery. The faces are softer and more gentle. The sculptor populates his heaven with idealized human beings who suggest a bliss quite unknown to early Buddhist thought.

The face of Buddha is long, the neck slender and the shoulders sloping. A heavy dress falls symmetrically over both shoulders and the sculptors concentrated on its

89

rhythms and folds. It must be remembered that in AD 486 the Emperor decreed that the court should wear Chinese rather than nomadic dress and this further step in the sinicization of the northern tribes was rapidly reflected in the sculptures of Yün-kang. From then onwards and particularly after 495, when the capital was moved from Ta-t'ung, this style of drapery became predominant, though sculptures in the older style were still occasionally produced. The effect, especially where the folds hang in series over the pedestals, is more graceful and decorative. The artists are thus more concerned with the whole figure and its effect than with just the upper half. The attendant figures with their sweeping robes ending in wing-like forms, and the crossed sashes low in the body, are typically Chinese and show the Chinese artists' preoccupation with graceful swirling clothes and the need to manage them discreetly. By comparison with earlier work, this is an art of great sophistication.

A Japanese art historian has pointed out that the clear light and crisp atmosphere of north China emphasize the lines of objects rather than their mass and attributes the Chinese love of line to this natural phenomenon.★ In addition it can be argued that Central Asian painting is essentially linear and in draped figures the Chinese were able to confine their love of line and movement without the restrictions which the nude figure imposed on them. The Chinese tradition is strong, and it is a tradition which encourages experiment. The Chinese in later Yün-kang workmanship are seeking a discreet intimacy with gods of native model rather than a monumentality and strangeness which would impress the spectator with the power of the unfamiliar. It shows a new confidence and in returning to the principal stream of Chinese art a delight in human experience. The delicacy of contours and the effortlessness of such figures suggest divinities which are not so much removed from their own world as, in the full spirit of mahāyāna Buddhism, sharing its experiences. Buddhism has become a Chinese religion, its gods are Chinese and the faithful will earn a Chinese paradise. The message is one of universal beauty rather than universal religious meaning.

Y. Yashiro: 2,000 Years of Japanese Art. London, 1958.

Notes on the plates on page 101

37

NOTES ON THE PLATES TO CHAPTER III

30   CENTRAL BUDDHA in Cave XX, *c.* AD 460–470. Height of head 4.10 m (13 $^1/_2'$). See also *plate 33,* and *pp. 74 ff., 81, 84.*

31   ATTENDANT BODHISATTVA to the right of the central Buddha in Cave XVIII, *c.* AD 460–470. See *pp. 74 ff., 85.*

32   ATTENDANT BODHISATTVA to the left of the central Buddha in Cave XVIII. See *pp. 74 ff., 85.*

33   GENERAL VIEW of a section of the Yün-kang cliffs constituting from right to left Caves XX–XXV. Height of the main seated Buddha in Cave XX, 13.44 m (44'). See *pp. 74 ff., 81, 83–85.*

34   VISNU IN HIGH RELIEF on the west reveal of the entrance arch of Cave VIII, *c.* AD 465–470. See *pp. 74 ff., 87.*

35   MANY-ARMED-AND-HEADED FIGURE in relief on the east reveal of the entrance arch of Cave VII, *c.* AD 465–470. See *pp. 74 ff., 88.*

36   GENERAL VIEW onto the back wall of Cave XV a. The figure missing from the central niche is in the Metropolitan Museum, New York, *c.* AD 465–470. See *pp. 74 ff., 83, 89.*

37   SEATED BODHISATTVA in the back wall of Cave XV a beside the central niche—detail of *plate 36.* This and the rest of the upper two rows of niches in this cave were carved *c.* AD 486–496, the lowest row was carved *c.* 500. See *pp. 74 ff., 83, 89.*

38   UPPER PART of the attendant bodhisattva in Cave XVIII to the left of the central Buddha. Surrounding it are five of the ten disciples of Sākyamuni Buddha, the other five are on the wall opposite. See *plate 32,* and *pp. 74 ff., 85, 110, 132.*

IV LUNG-MÊN

IN AD 493 Emperor Hsiao-wên of the Northern Wei dynasty decided to move the site of his capital from Ta-t'ung in Shansi near the Great Wall, south some 500 miles, to Lo-yang in Honan. The nomad population was always quite small compared with the Chinese they governed and during the early years of the dynasty they naturally felt insecure. Ta-t'ung was in the north and near the traditional home of the nomad peoples so that strategically it formed a suitable headquarters. As the Northern Wei became increasingly Chinese in blood and outlook, so political pressure to move the capital to a more central site increased. However, even by the end of the 5th century opposition to the plan still existed. Some of the more conservative nomads argued that the natives in those areas where Chinese traditions had been less disturbed would scorn their 'barbarian' origin. Such an attitude shows how Chinese they had become. Perhaps less reasonably they suggested that the different water and soil might bring diseases on them. Justifiably they also feared the rise of other nomad peoples of similar origin to their own—nomad tribes like the Jüan-jüan who, following in their own footsteps would be able to attack them through the areas they were leaving less guarded. Ta-t'ung had been an admirable base for a nomad people uncertain of their position. From it they had been able to control Shansi, Hopei and Shensi. The Yellow River had given them access to Kansu. Thus, they had been able to keep a watchful eye on all sources of possible trouble. They were now burning their boats.

The move to Lo-yang was an outward sign not only of increased responsibilities but also of the newcomers' complete surrender to Chinese culture. At the same time it advertised wider ambitions to fulfil what they considered to be their destiny, that of uniting and governing the whole of China. Lo-yang was one of China's oldest cities and had been a capital well over a thousand years before. More important historically—and the Chinese set great store by historical precedent—it had been the capital of the Later Han dynasty (AD 25–221). If the Northern Wei were to be considered throughout China as the true inheritors both politically and culturally of the Han, Lo-yang was a logical choice. In the chaotic centuries following the fall of the Later Han it had suffered badly. It was invaded in 303, 304 and 307, 308 and 310. The Hsiung-nu had occupied the city in 311, and only five years later it had been sacked and burned, its fine libraries destroyed and its sites left desolate. In 315 the tombs of some of the Han emperors were plundered. Now it was to be restored by just those barbarian people whom the Han had fought to exclude.

When the move was completed Ta-t'ung became little more than a provincial centre. However, it was never completely deserted. Monasteries continued their religious practices there undisturbed and some minor works went on in the Yün-kang caves. But Lo-yang became the main political, religious and artistic centre of activity.

The Northern Wei were not destined to enjoy their new capital for long un-disturbed. The city was sacked in 530 by discontented T'o-pa tribes and the Chinese element surviving this disaster established what they called the Eastern Wei dynasty (534–550) at another capital called Yeh. Still another faction established the Western Wei with a capital some 400 miles to the west at Ch'ang-an. This survived until 557. They were followed in rapid succession by the Northern Ch'i (550–577) and the Northern Chou (558–581)—short-lived dynasties which were of little power or prestige. Apart from some beautiful Buddhist sculpture, they left little mark on the history of China. In the south, the Liang dynasty with its court at Nanking continued to patronize Buddhism, especially under the devout Emperor Wu (502–549). Finally, in 589, a Chinese general Yang Chien, son-in-law of the last ruler of the Northern Chou, ended the confusion of these centuries by uniting both the north and south. The Sui dynasty which he founded was thrown away by a profligate son, but it served as an essential short prelude to the great T'ang dynasty (618–907).

Li Shih-min, who salvaged the Empire and founded his illustrious house, sprang from a noble Chinese family and was universally accepted as fit to occupy the throne. His wise and firm direction laid the foundations of one of the most glorious periods in Chinese and world history. The T'ang Empire at its height was greater and more influential than that of the Han. Its capital at Ch'ang-an, resplendent with temples, parks and palaces was the finest city in the world of that time. Especially during the first 150 years, the T'ang Chinese produced a flowering of the human spirit in the arts which is one of the most remarkable achievements of mankind. To read the poetry of a whole galaxy of T'ang writers is to be transformed to a scene where acute sensibilities and fine emotions are revealed against a background of wealth and

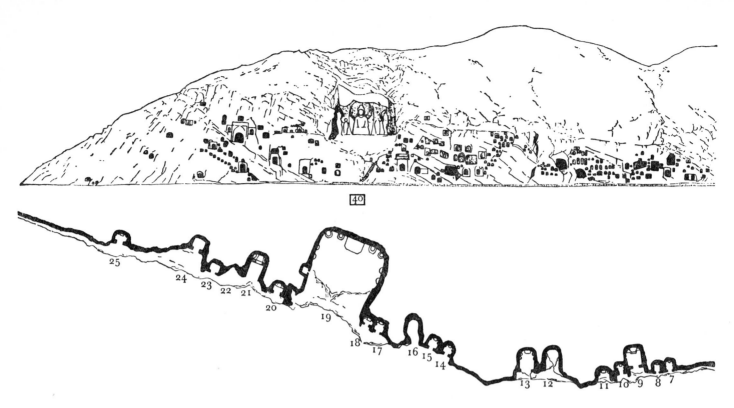

40

9 Plan and elevation of the 25 cave-temples of the Lung-mên group, Honan province. See plate 40.

power and energy. China became for the whole Far East what Greece and Rome had been for the West. People of many nations and religious beliefs found welcome and tolerance within the vast boundaries of a nation curious about innovations and confident in its ability not to be disturbed by them. The key routes across Central Asia were once again securely in Chinese hands. The nomads in the north were thoroughly cowed and gave no more trouble for nearly three centuries. The flow of religious knowledge kept pace with the increased trade across Central Asia. Li Shih-min, or to give him his imperial name, Emperor T'ai-tsung (627–650), encouraged the Buddhist faith. So also did his successors Kao-tsung (684–705) and the remarkable woman ruler Empress Wu. Despite her unscrupulous and even immoral behaviour she spent a vast sum on temples and their sculptures. She even liked her subjects to consider her a reincarnation of a bodhisattva.

The general conception of the cave temples near Lo-yang was the same as at Yün-kang. The River I, a tributary of the Yellow River, here cuts its way through a range of sandstone rock hills to form Lung-mên, 'The Dragon Gate'. The scale of the site can be appreciated from the general view in *plate 40* taken from the eastern side of the river looking at the western cliff in which the majority of the

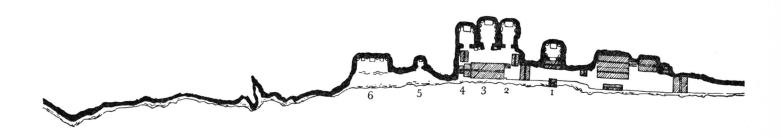

caves were cut from 495 onwards. From this distance one gains a true idea of the
size of the main shrine, the Fêng-hsien temple, with its row of huge statues. Originally the huge niche, 98 feet deep and 98 wide, was protected by a wooden structure
long since collapsed. An inscription on the throne of the central figure states that it
was begun on April 1st, 672, and completed on December 30th, 675. However, the
T'ang workmen may have inherited some of the groundwork, for as early as
AD 500 a huge cave had been started but was abandoned when two-thirds of its
height had been excavated. The Fêng-hsien cave probably occupies the site of this
unfinished Northern Wei shrine.

The central figure is a huge seated Buddha measuring 52 ft. 6 in. from the top of
the nimbus to the ground. It is seated on a lotus throne 9 ft. 9 in. high. The identity
of this particular figure presents some problems. Most authorities, on the basis of
an inscription dated AD 723, have identified it as Vairocana. This Buddha is not a
historical personality like Sākyamuni nor a saviour like Amitābha. Rather the figure
is symbolical of a universal principle for, according to late Mahāyāna doctrine, it
represents the original creative spirit behind the whole of creation. From this Buddha
spring a myriad Buddhas of a million worlds. In this hierarchy Sākyamuni is con-

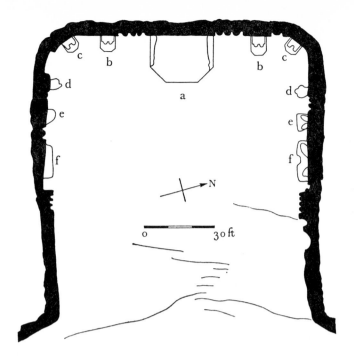

10 Plan of Fêng-hsien cave, Lung-mên. The seated Buddha at the back wall (a) is surrounded by symmetrically arranged figures: two lohans (b), two bodhisattvas (c), two acolytes (d), two heavenly kings (e), and two dvārapālas (f).

sidered as only a manifestation of Vairocana in one world. Vairocana remains the supreme, universal omnipresent Buddha. The principal text of this school of thought, in Chinese 'Hua-yen', was the lengthy *Avatamsaka Sūtra* which was first translated into Chinese in the beginning of the 5th century by the Kashmiran scholar Buddha-bhadra and retranslated in the 7th century by a scholar from Khotan. It is impossible to repeat here much of what, in translation, 'would fill a thousand-page encyclo-paedia', but one short quotation may help to indicate its general attitude.

Tatāgata is a synonym for the Buddha.

'The pure and wonderful Essence Body
Manifests its self-dependent power.
Throughout innumerable worldly realms
It shows forth the Tatāgata's body,★
Preaching widely the excellent Doctrine . . .
Its transformation bodies are countless,
Appearing everywhere in all regions . . .'★

R. Robinson: *Chinese Buddhist Verse*. London, 1954, pp. 53–54.

According to this doctrine the Variocana Buddha dwells upon a lotus-flower of a thousand petals. Each petal of this represents a universe and in each universe there are a myriad worlds, each with its Buddha. All of these are manifestations of the Buddha Principle. Despite its highly metaphysical approach the text made a certain appeal to Far Eastern imperial households. In Japan, in particular, the Emperor liked to make an analogy in which he considered himself as the worldly equivalent of the central Vairocana while the large Buddha figures on the lotus leaves were his high officers and the tiny Buddha figures represented his subjects.★ The 7th century in China was a critical period for the introduction and spread of new sects and one must allow a certain time lag for these new beliefs to reach Japan. The *Avatamsaka Sūtra* was brought to Japan from China in AD 736, and this makes it quite possible that the text and its Vairocana Buddha idea were familiar in mid-7th century China.

G. Sansom: *A Short Cultural History of Japan*. London, 1946, p. 126.

However, it is open to question whether at this time the Chinese would have dedicated such a huge central figure dominating the Lung-mên complex to a comparatively new aspect of Buddhism, rarely understood by the average worshipper. The most popular Buddha of the period was undoubtedly Amitābha who presided over the Western Paradise. This belief came into China quite early but did not gain wide popularity until the time of the famous monk translator Kumārajīva who worked in China from 383 to 413. Amitābha is unknown to early Buddhist dogma. It is a Buddha born of a lotus in the Western Paradise. As a bodhisattva his words are included in the basic text of the school, the *Sukhavūti-Vyūha Sūtra*.

> '*When I have become a Buddha*
> *May my country be the highest,*
> *Its people rare and excellent,*
> *Its field-of-truth superlative,*
> *The land as good as Nirvāṇa,*
> *Matchless and incomparable.*
> *Then in pity and compassion*
> *I will liberate all beings.*
> *Men from ten quarters who, reborn,*
> *Their hearts rejoicing and unstained,*
> *Have arrived inside my country*
> *Will dwell in peace and happiness.*'★

R. Robinson. Ibid., p. 43.

What made this belief particularly popular was the comparative ease with which the believer could attain salvation. He need only sincerely invoke the name of Amitābha. It can readily be appreciated that this doctrine made an immediate appeal to everyday people for whom the more profound aspects of Buddhism were too abstruse. This was the type of Buddhism that was destined to outstrip all others in popularity. W. Willetts has suggested that what was originally an Amitābha group when created in the mid-7th century at Lung-mên may have been dedicated afresh when Vairocana became a popular belief in the first decades of the 8th century.★

W. Willetts: in *Illustrated London News*. February 1954, pp. 187-188.

The group originally contained nine huge figures in all. On each side of the central Buddha stand an arhat followed by a bodhisattva. The walls then turn at right angles to the back of the cave and each side thus formed is occupied by a *lokapāla* and a *dvārapāla*. *Plate 41* shows the pair on the north wall. Lokapālas protect the four quarters of space. They are the guardians of the world and of the Buddhist faith and as such are frequently found at the entrances to Buddhist temples. Dvārapālas are powerful men, heroes, demigods who fulfil the same protective function as the lokapālas. Much confusion exists in identifying these divinities and their development from Indian models. The lokapāla on the left holding a model stūpa in his right hand and with his left hand on his waist is identified from an inscription as Vaisravana. His right foot rests in the head of one of his subjects, a dwarf of whom he is king. The cult of Vaisravana became popular in the mid-7th century and a temple was built to him. He was canonized as the Chinese God of Wealth in 653.★ Similar figures made of glazed clay are found in many T'ang tombs.

The peaceful conditions which T'ang arms established in Central Asia encouraged the interchange of religious knowledge and more Chinese priests went to India in the 7th century than at any other period. At times the Chinese emperors even actively encouraged the travellers. The search for manuscripts, images and relics to bring back to China went on unceasingly and Chinese curiosity extended to many hitherto unexplored aspects of Indian culture such as Brahmanical philosophy, astronomy and mathematics.

By far the most famous of all Chinese travellers was Hsüan-tsang. He was born of a noble family in A D 600 and at twenty he was ordained. Dissatisfied with existing translations of the sacred texts, in 629 he secretly left China for India. Reaching India by the northern route he spent sixteen years travelling throughout the sub-continent including Nepal and Ceylon. He studied under the most famous teachers of the time and finally returned to China in 645 after a journey of some 20,000 miles. He worked until his death in 664 to translate the sūtras he had collected, train students and found temples. At the request of the Emperor he wrote a record of his travels which greatly inspired interest in India and the lands between.

India at this time was under the Gupta dynasty which is generally reckoned as lasting from 320 and is reckoned to end with the reign of King Harsha of Kanauji who died in 647. The India which Hsüan-tsang described was united as it had not been since Mauryan times in the 3rd century B C. It abounded in splendid monasteries and stūpas. Its universities, like that of Nālanda, were famous for their wide learning. With the decay of western influences, its art had returned to gather the full harvest

W. Willetts. Ibid.

of its native ideals. Rowland says of this period, 'Seldom in the history of people do we find a period in which the national genius is so fully and typically expressed in all the arts as in Gupta India. Here was florescence and fulfilment after a long period of gradual development, a like sophistication and complete assurance of expression ... a norm or degree of perfection never achieved before or since, and in the perfect balance and harmony of all elements stylistic and iconographic...'* The land was rich and the wealthy men patronized and practised the arts. With two great dynasties in power and the routes between them secure, conditions were ideal for the art and teachings of India to spread throughout the whole of the Far East.

B. Rowland: The Art and Architecture of India. London, 1935, p. 130.

Hsüan-tsang brought seven Gupta figures back to China from his travels in India. The 7th and 8th centuries were the critical period for the new influences from India on Chinese workmanship, and the Chinese sculptors seem to have surrendered momentarily to them. Even at this distance one can sense the tremor of delight with which the Chinese in the luxury of the 7th century saw Gupta images—after the impassive planes of early Yün-kang torsos and the heavy concealing drapery of late Northern Wei figures, diaphanous draperies reveal the soft lines and warm flesh of living, physically desirable beings.

The central seated Buddha is very different from the Northern Wei types. Even in such a noble and spiritual figure the heavy dignity of the early Wei, and the mystical spirit of the later Wei figures have surrendered to the appeal of rich, warm humanity. The drapery once more becomes thin, covering the body without stifling it. The decorative values of hanging drapery are of less importance than the living humanity beneath. The face and neck are round and fleshy, the expression calm, but the lips and eyes are very much of this world. No Buddha figure would, of course, be allowed jewellery, but the sculptor has beautified the central figure by a most ornate and splendid background of flaming halo and nimbus which sweep from almost floor level to above the head. The Chinese with their gift for compromise have produced a figure which is calm and full of repose. It stresses neither of the two Indian extremes, asceticism and sensuality. It harmonizes rather than transcends human desires. The face is personalized, the drapery clings naturally, its decorative effect being only a secondary condition. The sense of space is developed by making the figures more fully in the round than hitherto.

Plate 39

The new sculptural influences coming from Gupta India are seen fully developed in the attendant figures and lokapālas. Here the sculptors felt free of the restraint which the traditions of Buddha figures imposed on them. With their threatening postures they make a perfect foil to the calm Buddha and the all-compassionate bodhisattvas.

Plates 41, 42, 43

The living, moving quality is emphasized in such a way that the function of guarding is vividly portrayed. One feels that here is Buddhism militant.

In China as in Gupta India the human body became the principal theme for religious sculpture. The sculptors refined it and idealized it so that it was not without reason that a T'ang purist complained the bodhisattvas looked like dancing girls. The tendency is seen at its most developed in the powerful figure on the right of *plate 41*. This dvārapāla originated from an Indian model, for such guardians are found on the railings of Buddhist stūpas from early times and are some of the most impressive works remaining from this period of Buddhist art in India.* The muscles of abdomen and neck stand out strongly to emphasize the terrifying aspect of the face. The strings of jewels and the soft swinging folds of the *dhoti* emphasize the muscular strength of the huge torso and at the same time bring added life and movement. It is important to appreciate a fundamental difference between Indian and Chinese use of drapery. The Indians use it generally to emphasize the form beneath. The Chinese, true to their traditions, use it to emphasize movement. The widely separated legs planted firmly on the ground add power to the defensive position of this protector of the door. For all its latent power and muscular contortion the figure has a certain controlled poise, a restraint which increases its effect. The sculptor was not seeking, as did the Greeks, the expression of the human body in movement and hoping to infuse a life-giving force into it. He was trying to express a superhuman power, expressed in superhuman muscular terms. At the same time we see combined the strength and weakness of Chinese sculpture—an uneasiness with the naked body which can amount to clumsiness, a skill with drapery which overcomes all difficulties and can beautify even the grotesque. Even in such extravagant figures, symbols of energy, one sees the Chinese artist with his love of movement and economy of line choosing just those aspects of Indian art in which he could excel. But the Chinese soon abandoned this over-explicit style leaving the Japanese to develop it.

When one travels through the cave temples of China one is naturally impressed by the endless repetitions of similar religious types, expressing no emotional qualities in its main figures on the one hand and devoted to strict iconographical truth to type on the other. Only rarely does one find in, for instance, the early Yün-kang caves glimpses of individuality, and then it is in minor attendant figures such as arhats. The outstanding early example of this is seen in *plate 38* where the emaciated face of a disciple looks out from the wall on the upper left of the main figure in striking contrast to the other impersonal deities.

H. Zimmer and J. Campbell: *The Art of India Asia.* New York, 1955, p. 163.

The T'ang dynasty saw a notable increase in the art of portraiture. The most impressive examples which have survived are clay tomb figures (see Chapter VII), some of remarkable size. They range from dancing girls to priests, from Central Asian attendants and dwarf entertainers to Confucian dignitaries. A period which set great store by the material benefits of this world naturally also paid considerable attention to personalities. In the T'ang period for the first time we deal with people who seem really alive. The poets of this period, for example, are remarkably personalized. We remember a person for his eccentricities and the T'ang centuries produced many outstanding men in all walks of life.

Buddhist craftsmen naturally found it difficult to pay great attention to the peculiarities of the flesh when dealing with the main Buddha figures, but in the figures of priests and disciples one feels that one is concerned with real people.

In the cliff opposite that containing the Fêng-hsien-ssu, are a smaller number of caves, the most famous being the K'an-ching-ssu. The meaning of this term is not known and it is so-called from an inscription on the outside of the cave dated 1769. The central figure is a seated Buddha, but more interesting is the row of arhats carved *Plate 45* in fairly shallow relief round three walls. They are arranged in such a way as to give *Plates 44, 46* the impression of a procession.

Great variety is given to these figures by a variation of hand gesture, angle of the head and cast of feature. Each is a rare study in portraiture. Most of the figures appear to be Indian and perhaps Central Asian, but some are Chinese.

Man in art emerged in the Han dynasty and from that time Chinese artists had been struggling with the problems of depicting personality—especially in the tombs. The introduction of Indian art and particularly of the arhat and the donor gave a great impetus to Chinese artists to experiment in the medium. It is open to question if they succeeded except in such rare instances as are here illustrated. It was left to the Japanese to take up the form with brilliant success.

Notes on the plates on page 123

42

43

NOTES ON THE PLATES TO CHAPTER IV

39   THE MAIN SEATED BUDDHA AND A LOHAN in Fêng-hsien temple, AD 672–675. See *figure 10*, and *pp. 107, 109.*

40   GENERAL VIEW of the Lung-mên cliff from across the River I. See *figure 9*, and *p. 104.*

41   FROM LEFT TO RIGHT, bodhisattva and two guardian figures (a heavenly king and a dvārapāla) ranged to the central Buddha's left in Fêng-hsien temple, AD 672–675. See *figure 10*, and *pp. 108–110, 163.*

42   DETAIL of the heavenly king in *plate 41*.

43   DETAIL of the dvārapāla in *plate 41*.

44   THE RIGHT-HAND WALL of the K'an-ching temple with its frieze of arhats in relief which continues around the two other walls of the temple. Mid-T'ang dynasty. See *p. 111.*

45   MAIN SEATED BUDDHA of the K'an-ching temple. See *p. 111.*

46   TWO ARHATS from the relief frieze on the left wall of the K'an-ching temple. See *p. 111.*

V TUN-HUANG

THE CAVES of the Thousand Buddhas near Tun-huang are the oldest of all the Chinese cave temples. Work was started on them in the second half of the 4th century AD, about a century before the Northern Wei emperors adopted the Buddhist faith and began excavating the Yün-kang caves. The site is the oldest surviving monument to the faith which changed the life of the East as much as Christianity did that of the West, but nothing of this earliest pre-Yün-kang period at Tun-huang remains, which is the reason for its being presented here, later than Yün-kang and Lung-mên.

The City of Tun-huang, as opposed to the Caves, was founded in 111 BC during the reign of Emperor Wu of the Han dynasty. From this time it has occupied a very particular position in Chinese history. It is an oasis in the deserts of western Kansu, a neck of land stretching into the approaches to Central Asia with Tibet to its south and Mongolia to the north. It is a bleak and vulnerable spot, but to the early travellers from India and Central Asia it meant the end of their long trials. At Tun-huang the caravans finally entered the first town of China proper. It was here that those leaving the safety of the Middle Kingdom en route to the west, made their last preparations for the long and dangerous journey ahead. Leaving China, the caravans had then to travel slowly either north of the T'ien mountains across the Gobi desert, or south of them through the Tarim basin to Kashgar and Khotan, no less than 1,200 miles away. The route was not a new one, for the missionaries and merchants were following the old trade routes across Central Asia by which in Han times the silk of China had reached the Roman Empire. The Tun-huang area was an ideal meeting place for the cultures of China and of the lands bordering Central Asia.

Tun-huang, or, as it is sometimes called, Sha-chou, 'The City of Sands', was the great western strategic outpost of the Chinese Empire. At certain times during the Han dynasty it formed the pivot of the western end of the Great Wall, and, some 70 miles beyond, its forts stretched into the desert to give early warning of approaching invaders. As early as those first centuries AD a strong garrison was based on this oasis town and the Chinese armies which set out on their expeditions into Central Asia assembled there. We encountered it in Han times when General Li Kuang-li, in disgrace after his return from his unsuccessful expedition into Central Asia, was ordered to camp outside Tun-huang and await a decision on his fate. Finally he was given a second chance, and reinforcements were sent for a second and, this time, successful attempt. After his expedition of 102 to 101 B C the fortifications of the Great Wall were pushed out beyond Tun-huang, and the Great Wall for the first time began to fulfil an offensive rather than a defensive function.

Thus, in the first centuries of our era, Tun-huang guarded what was the most important trade and military route between China and East Turkestan. China's ambitions in Central Asia depended upon the safe control of this once large oasis along the natural high-road to the west. Fed by the Tang-ho River which comes from the Western Nan-shan mountains, some of whose peaks are covered with perpetual snow, at its period of greatest prosperity the Tun-huang oasis covered an area 20 miles from north to south and 16 miles at its widest. The introduction of improved agricultural techniques in the 3rd century, attributed to an energetic local governor Huang-fu Lung, increased the prosperity and economic independence of the area.★ No other settlement in the area was comparable in size and importance.

E. Zürcher: *The Buddhist Conquest of China*. Leiden, 1959, pp. 59 and 339.

The town has suffered over the centuries. After the revolt of An Lu-shan in the T'ang dynasty (AD 755), the central government was no longer able to control the provincial armies effectively and the borders were at the mercy of barbarian attack. The Tibetans were particularly dangerous, and in 759 they captured Tun-huang, occupying it for nearly a century. The Hsi-hsia, or Tanguts, a tribe related to the Tibetans, occupied it throughout the 11th and 12th centuries. Again in the mid-19th century the Tungan rebels did serious damage in the area. Buddhism too was not always in favour at the Chinese court, persecutions of the faith diminished the importance of Tun-huang as a centre of religious activity. The possibilities of the river for irrigation purposes are not now used to the full and the oasis has shrunk.

Perhaps the most amazing feature of the Caves of the Thousand Buddhas is that so much has survived at all in such a vulnerable area. The almost universal esteem in which the Buddhist faith was held no doubt accounted for its comparative safety from hostile men. Through the centuries the piety of a number of wealthy families led to restorations, and at all times the inhabitants of the area were not unmindful of the wealth that the pilgrims brought to this otherwise uninviting area. Perhaps most important of all, the climate of the district, with its almost complete absence of rain, has protected the site and especially the wall paintings from the kind of damage from the elements which has destroyed most of the other evidence of a once great and widespread art.

The Chinese at all times regarded the place as the back-of-beyond and to be sent there on military service meant little short of exile. Chinese poetry is full of references to the miseries of the place. A poet of the T'ang dynasty writes,

Liu Chung-yung. Trans. S. Jenyns: *Selections from 300 Poems of the T'ang dynasty.* London, 1946, p. 99.

'*Year by year if it is not the Golden River it is the Jade Door Pass;*
Morning after morning we take up our whips and gird on our sword rings.
Through the white snow of three springs we have buried our dead comrades
*   in "green tombs" of exile*
Where for ten thousand li the Yellow River winds its way through
*   the Black Hills.*'*

But like all frontier posts there was an element of romance attached to it and behind many of the sad lines, one senses the fascination of the unknown which lay beyond the deserts and the mountains. A caravan might arrive from India or further west bringing strange luxuries or men of holiness and learning; on the other hand a savage tribe might sweep in from the lands to the north to threaten the prosperity of the Middle Kingdom. Unknown political changes in the far west might have their repercussions on the frontiers of China.

Li Po: 'The Moon in the Mountain Pass'. Ibid.

'*From ancient times was this a battle ground*
Whence none returned.
The soldiers gaze to far horizons
And many sad faces think of homesteads left behind.'*

We have already seen how the Yün-kang caves owed their origin to the inspiration of the pious monk T'an-yao. The caves of Tun-huang also owe their beginnings to a 4th-century monk named Lo-tsun. In the small museum of the Tun-huang Research Institute is a stone inscription of 698 which tells how this monk Lo-tsun once found himself in the vicinity when suddenly the rays of the setting sun bathed three peaks of the hills in a red light. From the top of the peaks countless golden rays emanated and within them a thousand shapes appeared. He took this as divine inspiration and forthwith began the excavation of caves in the face of the cliff opposite the range of hills.

Buddhism at this time was spreading rapidly, especially in the north, but it must have been of a comparatively 'primitive' type, a mixture of hinayāna, mahāyāna and native ideas and practices which could be incorporated into the faith. The great translators were already at work on the vast corpus of Buddhist writing, especially

mahāyāna, produced in the three centuries before AD 200. The Indo-Scythian Dharmarakṣa, born *c.* 230, was active about 266–308 and was well versed in the Chinese
classics as well as in the Buddhist scriptures—an ideal man to propagate the faith
among the Chinese. He travelled widely in Central Asia and finally settled in Ch'ang-
an where he devoted his life to the translation of the mahāyāna classics. Seventy-two
of his translations have survived and he justly ranks as one of the foremost founders
of Buddhism in China. His work was ably continued by one of the most famous
translators, Kumārajīva, who was active in Ch'ang-an from 402 onwards. Kumārajīva translated the famous *Lotus Sūtra* and travelled frequently between Ch'ang-an
and Tun-huang where his pupil Fu-chêng had a monastery and a school of translators. We learn that the first Chinese to penetrate into Central Asia in search of
Buddhist learning was a certain Chu Shih-hsing who went to Khotan probably as
early as AD 260.★ The oasis of Tun-huang must indeed have been a very cosmopolitan place in these early centuries and its population was probably more Central
Asian than Chinese. The pilgrims must have added colour and an international flavour.
In the 3rd century embassies and tribute came from Lopnor, Khotan, Kucha, Qara-
sāhr and Ferghana to Lo-yang, capital of the Western Chin dynasty (265–317).★

E. Zürcher: op. cit., p. 61.

Ibid. I am much indebted to
this fine study for some of the
details of early Buddhism in
China.

The caves were started in a period when the area enjoyed comparative peace,
but when the country elsewhere was passing through troubled times. The comparatively stable dictatorship of the Ts'ao family (220–265) was followed by the
Western Chin dynasty (265–317) during which Buddhism flourished in the west.
But from about 300 warfare throughout the land made conditions more difficult.
The faith still made steady progress; but it was not until the arrival of the Northern
Wei dynasty in the 4th century that settled conditions came to the area and Buddhism entered upon its period of greatest expansion. As Conze remarks, 'To a
person who is thoroughly disillusioned with the contemporary world and with himself, Buddhism may offer many points of attraction—in the transcending sublimity
of the fairyland of its subtle thoughts, in the splendour of its works of art, in the
magnificence of its hold over vast population, and in the determined heroism and
great refinement of those who are steeped into it.'★

E. Conze: *Buddhism*. Oxford,
1951, p. 13.

During this period of political confusion, the pomp and glory of the Han were
always cherished memories. Like the Northern Wei later, each of the ephemeral
powers which held sway in north China seems to have dreamed of re-establishing
at least its military grandeur. Buddhism, the only civilizing influence in the north
of China, somehow not only survived but flourished, and we learn that, when the
Northern Wei captured the area, they moved no less than 30,000 Buddhist families

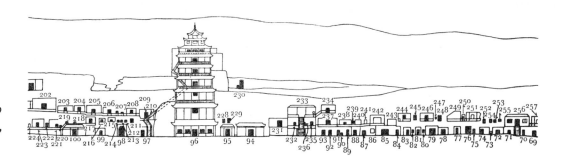

11 *Elevation of part of the group of cave-temples at Tun-huang, Kansu province.*

to their new capital at P'ing-ch'êng. To most of the barbarian kingdoms, the Buddhist missionaries, though men of culture, must have appeared harmless, humble and trustworthy by comparison with the remnants of China's traditional leaders.

As it now stands, the cliff face into which the caves are carved measures 1¼ miles from north to south and contains no less than 480 caves. In the last few years the Tun-huang Research Institute under its devoted Director Chang Shu-hung has done most valuable work in preserving what remains of the caves and in clearing those which had filled with drifting sand. In earlier times, the caves, placed at different levels in the cliff face, were connected by wooden platforms and walks. Many of these had collapsed and are only now being replaced. Thus the visitor can at present see more of the works of these caves than for many centuries past. The Research Institute is slowly publishing its finds, and one hopes that eventually we shall have the kind of documentation for Tun-huang that Japanese scholars made for Yün-kang. Meanwhile much remains tentative and unexplored.

Although the site of the Tun-huang caves has always been well known to countless eastern travellers, it was the exploration of Sir Aurel Stein in 1907 that first revealed it to the West. He had heard that a Taoist monk two years previously had discovered a huge hoard of manuscripts said to be hidden in a secret chamber and was determined to gain access to them. The monk custodian was extremely suspicious and had bricked up the door to this chamber. Stein recognized the danger of antagonizing a local population which was deeply attached to the shrines. The cave leading to the secret room was in charge of this humble Taoist monk who had taken on himself the task of restoring it, unfortunately in execrable taste, to what he thought was its former splendour. The find had previously been reported to the central government which, however, seemed little interested in the documents. Only Stein's guile, diplomacy and finally the offer of a large contribution to the temple restoration fund gained him access to the walled-up room. Claiming spiritual kinship with the great Chinese Buddhist traveller Hsüan-tsang, he finally gained the priest's complete confidence and, as a consequence, was able to carry away twenty-

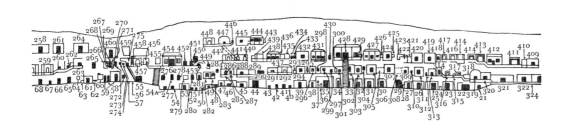

nine heavy packing cases of manuscripts, some nine thousand in Chinese alone and hundreds in many rare Central Asian and Indian scripts. His loot included many beautiful paintings on silk, and embroideries, tapestries, etc., which were divided between the British Museum and the Indian Museum. A year later, Professor Paul Pelliot of the Sorbonne visited the shrine and was able to buy many more documents from the cache and these are now in Paris. Taken together they throw much light on the little known languages of Central Asia and on the Buddhist and Manichaean religions of the huge area between India and China. The chamber seems to have been walled up sometime after the middle of the 10th century, and the documents date from the 7th to 10th centuries.

Much still remained after Pelliot's visit and Chinese scholars then awoke to the importance of the find. Orders were issued for the remains to be shipped to Peking, but much of the money for this disappeared *en route* to Tun-huang and many of the manuscripts disappeared from the hastily packed carts on the way back. It seems that very little reached Peking. However, the monk had held back a considerable reserve. The Japanese bought some in 1911, and the rest Stein was able to buy in 1914. At the same time he was able to purchase many documents which had been pilfered on the way to Peking. This discovery of paintings, textiles and documents is the largest corpus of works dating to this early period which has been made and is of the utmost interest for linguistic, religious and art studies.★ Professor Pelliot published six volumes of photographs of the caves themselves, which have remained our chief source of knowledge ever since. Unfortunately no text appeared.★ More recently the Tun-huang Institute have published excellent copies of the wall paintings★ and one or two travellers have obtained colour photographs.★

Unlike at the Yün-kang and Lung-mên sites, the conglomerate type of rock formation at Tun-huang is unsuitable for sculpture. As a result of the mixture of rock and clay which forms the cliff, the excavators were able to make only much smaller caves than at the other two sites. It is impossible to carve statues in this material, and the devotees were forced to make their icons of clay moulded round

Sir M. Aurel Stein: *Serindia. Detailed Report of Exploration in Central Asia and Westernmost China*, 4 Vols. Oxford, 1921. A more popular account in *Ruins of Desert Cathay*. London, 1912.

Paul Pelliot, *Mission Pelliot en Asie Centrale: Les grottes de Touen Houang*. 6 Vols. plates. Paris, 1914–24. 'Une bibliothèque médiévale retrouvée au Kan-sou', *Revue des Arts Asiatiques*. Paris, 1908.

Chang Shu-hung: *Ton-ko no Heki-ga*, Tokyo, 1958.

Irene Vongehr Vincent: *The Sacred Oasis. Caves of the Thousand Buddhas. Tun-huang*. London, 1953.

a wooden armature. Such a technique tends to produce more plastic effects than are possible in stone and enabled the artists to give the faces more expression and the poses more sense of movement. Siren remarks that 'the modelling is here more sensitive than in most sculptures of the Northern Wei period known to us and the linear rhythm softly tempered'.* The figures were then highly coloured, and this added greatly to the naturalism.

Monumental sculpture in clay, which is a cheaper material than either stone or bronze, must have been common throughout the whole of China, especially during the T'ang dynasty. However, only at Tun-huang and Mai-chi-shan has any quantity survived. The familiar tomb figurines give evidence of a tremendous variety and invention on a smaller scale, but for other examples of a great monumental tradition we must look to Japan, where the large clay statues of the mid-8th century in such places as the Tōdai-ji at the old capital of Nara, could almost have been made in the same atelier. The menacing figure in *plate 68* and the nearest figure in *plate 67* are two of the Four Warrior Gods who guard the four cardinal directions of the Buddhist world. The Japanese figures of the same subjects are perhaps slightly simpler in their armour and decoration, but they show a direct knowledge of the religious art of contemporaneous China and show how quickly such types became common throughout the whole Far Eastern Buddhist world. As we mentioned in the chapter on Lung-mên, the mobility seen in the colossi of that site is the outcome of closer contact between China and India during T'ang times—dance-like poses, emphasized proportions, sensual figures—these were the innovations of the T'ang, brought directly back from India by travellers like Hsüan-tsang and Wang Hsüan-ts'ê. Movement in art has always appealed strongly to the Chinese who took up the Indian modes with enthusiasm and made of them a completely new art. It is as if the Chinese were now seeing the human body with new interest and heightened observation. The Indian imports did not completely Indianize Chinese art. The Chinese made their synthesis and achieved through it the most powerful and dynamic plastic expression that the Far East has ever known.*

Plates 61, 62, 65 and 66 are in a style created slightly earlier than that of the full T'ang. The Buddhas and bodhisattvas with their Thousand Buddhas painted on the walls behind them belong to the Sui period. This short period AD 589–618 was founded by General Yang Chien who succeeded in reuniting the north and south of China for the first time since Han times. Unfortunately his son destroyed his father's work by grandiose schemes of conquest and vast public works which over-taxed a nation only just recovering from centuries of warfare. A strange parallel

O. Siren: *Chinese Painting.* London, 1956. Vol. I, p. 64.

B. Rowland: 'Indian Images in Chinese Sculpture', *Artibus Asiae.* Vol. X, 1. 1947, p. 20.

exists between the First Emperor who built the Great Wall and Yang Chien who was responsible for the Grand Canal, a vast waterway linking north and south China, lined with trees and palaces, the work of millions of forced labourers.

The 6th century in Central Asia had been one of comparative peace under the control of the Turks, and Buddhism prospered. The Sui emperors made laws to protect Buddhist property and ordered the construction of nearly four thousand temples. The Tun-huang Institute records ninety-four Sui caves. Countless old statues were repaired and new ones ordered. Sui diplomacy returned to the Han pattern. It aimed at splitting the Turkish forces and by 608 the once dangerous Central Asian forces were divided, their great leaders dead and the Chinese able to occupy strategic oases in Central Asia such as Hami. Kansu in particular was safe and Tun-huang could share the national peace and prosperity. Diplomatic relations again became easy and the whole of the Far East was alive with new ideas. The Japanese went to China and, more important still, Chinese embassies went to India returning with lion skins, agate goblets, dancing girls and Buddhist sūtras.

The style of the Sui Buddhist statues marks another step in the freeing of Buddhist images from the all enveloping folds of monastic dress which dominated Chinese statues until the mid-6th century. The revelation of the form beneath the dress began to show itself in the sculpture of the Northern Ch'i (550–577) and Northern Chou dynasties (558–581). This was fundamentally due to the new influences coming into China from Gupta India. The serenity of the faces in the Sui is a human serenity, the brilliant decorations of the bodhisattva robes are such as would befit royalty. The graceful shape of the Buddha is visible beneath the thin robes—taken almost directly from wall paintings in Central Asian sites like Kucha which in their turn looked to Mathurā. The medieval quality has gone, so also the ecstasy. The bodhisattvas do not yet look like the dancing girls of the full T'ang style, but these painted figures show the relaxation better than the stone figures which have survived. The attendant bodhisattvas even show a slight tendency to the *tribangha* posture, the thrice bent movement, the waist to one side with one hip out-thrust and a slight lean forwards. This is the movement which gives later figures their gentle seductiveness. The elongated faces with their archaic smiles have disappeared with the clothing—it is indeed difficult to imagine any way in which they could have been combined.

We see the full T'ang style, the triumph of materialism over mysticism, in a whole range of figures in *plate 69* where many members of the family of Buddhist dramatis personae surround the central Buddha. Seated bodhisattvas, standing lohans and kneeling worshippers piously serve the main figure within a large painted niche. The impression is similar to that produced by a Christian nativity group. The painted figures are so arranged that they enlarge and give depth to the group of sculpted figures in a most naturalistic manner. The styles of painting and modelling correspond. The whole ceiling of the niche is taken up with another crowded composition of a Buddha in his heaven surrounded by a host of worshippers.

Plate 67 shows a guardian, a bodhisattva and a lohan, all also of the 8th century. The contrast between the emotional qualities of the figures is immediately visible—the rhythmic power of the guardian with his exaggerated pose and features, the feminine softness of the bodhisattva, detached and calm, the human asceticism of the lohan ever attentive and prayerful. The poses are fully relaxed, easy and natural without being loose. The special joy of the Buddhist sculptor in groups is here shown at its most fully developed. With all the techniques at his command he has sought a quiet but impressive intimacy and an expression of the perfect harmony which should exist within the Buddhist world. Even the suppressed violence of the guardian does not disturb the serenity of the composition.

The lohan figures are of particular interest in Chinese art for they gave the Chinese sculptor a rare opportunity for a more personal approach to the problems of depicting the human face. The lohan is one who has 'extirpated his passions' and was originally simply one who had comprehended the Four Truths. The term was then applied to the apostles, disciples or missionaries of the Buddha—the number being variously stated as ten, fifteen and even five hundred.

Plate 38 A group of ten such figures in the T'an-yao Cave XVIII are among the most interesting figures in the whole of Yün-kang. The individual features and striking personalities of their heads are quite unique and must be the earliest survivals of their type in Chinese art. There they form an effective foil to the somewhat stereotyped figures of Buddhas and bodhisattvas and the artists seem to have taken up the form with enthusiasm, certainly from the 6th century onwards. The masks of early Japanese sculpture fulfil a similar function. Perhaps their finest expression in China are the large glazed pottery figures of monks dating from the 10th to 13th centuries.

The earliest here represented from Tun-huang are the two figures on the right of the Buddha in *plate 59*. The heads are shown enlarged in *plates 57 and 58*. These belong to the early 7th century. Although it is very difficult to identify them with any certainty, a number of types became popular. The younger of the two may represent Ananda, the youngest and most handsome of the disciples, and the other probably Mahā-Kāśyapa, the oldest and most experienced. It was natural for the

Chinese artists to select these two easily identified and sharply contrasted personalities from the whole galaxy of disciples. The bodies and draperies are somewhat roughly executed, but the features repay closer study; the one youthful yet disciplined, the other deeply furrowed and set in the determination of his holy calling. These figures add a telling human element to the drama of Buddhist love.

These Tun-huang statues are unique in the whole of Far Eastern statuary for the amount of original painted decoration which has survived. Much of the original painting on the statues of Yün-kang has disappeared. In this respect the two bodhisattvas standing on either side of the Buddha in *plate 66* are very revealing. The bodhisattva standing on the Buddha's left wears a close fitting dress which comes down from the left shoulder, crosses the body and goes up under the right arm. The cloth is divided into diamond-shaped frames containing confronting phoenixes and flowers. Small rosettes are at the junctions of the frames. A number of textile patterns were imported across Central Asia from Sassanian art and these appear both in Tun-huang textiles and as far east as Japan, doubtless taken there by cultural missions to China in the 7th century. The phoenix design, although in a typical Sassanian setting, seems to be a Chinese innovation and a motif which was very popular in T'ang applied arts. The pattern here seems to be in a transitional stage and before its full development under the T'ang.★

B. Gray and J. B. Vincent: *Buddhist Cave Paintings at Tunhuang.* London, 1959, pp. 51–52.

The haloes of the figures are very richly painted. 'Around the body of the Buddha there is always a light, a fathom wide, on all sides which shines constantly day and night, as brilliantly as a thousand suns, and resembling a mountain of jewels in movement'★; and the thousands of tiny Buddha figures create a most impressive background. Their colours are varied and interspersed with ground mother-of-pearl haloes which must have glittered most impressively in the light of flickering torches. The group must have created a far greater impression than similar ones at Yün-kang which are generally represented by comparatively few niches, often lost within the mass of larger works or which are comparatively uninteresting by their lack of variety. It should be mentioned in passing that this probably was not the original position of the group but they were doubtless set up somewhere in this cave.

E. Conze, op. cit., p. 36.

The *mudrā*, or hand gestures, are somewhat unusual. The Chinese often departed from the canons of Indian iconography. The central Buddha has the right hand in the common *abhaya,* or gesture which banishes fear. The left hand held straight out palm upwards is probably a variant of the *vara mudrā,* the gesture of giving. The two attendant figures have no attributes by which to distinguish them and seem to be merely contemplative, calm figures who practise the meditation which is the

S. Mizuno and T. Nagahiro: *Yün-kang*. Vols. VIII and IX, Kyoto, 1953, p. 83.

most important Buddhist way to salvation. As at Yün-kang they have no definite personality—they could equally well be simple celestials.★ The identification of the central Buddha is difficult. It may be intended to represent Sākyamuni, the historical Buddha, but may equally well be intended as Amitābha, the Buddha who presides over the Western Paradise amidst souls reborn into it from lotus-flowers. During T'ang times Amitābha was by far the most popular of Buddhas. A few decades later Shan-tao, one of the most famous priests of the Pure Land sect, began the composition of his Evening Hymn of Praise

> '*Praise! We most sincerely dedicate our lives in worship*
> *To Amida (Amitābha) Buddha of the Western Quarter.*
> *The sea of Amida's wisdom and vow*
> *Is deep and broad, without shore or bottom,*
> *Those who hear his name and wish for rebirth*
> *Will each and every one reach his country.*
> *May all living beings be reborn in the land of Peace and Joy.*'★

R. Robinson: op. cit., p. 66.

Indeed, no more faithful representation of popular Mahāyāna Buddhism exists than at Tun-huang.

The Tun-huang caves have yet another claim to our attention. They contain on their walls the largest corpus of early Chinese painting which has survived. Twenty-two Wei caves have been identified and the wall paintings date back to this period, to before AD 500, when the Northern Wei emperors had just moved their capital and were engaged on the Lung-mên caves. Altogether the paintings in the caves span nearly one thousand years. *Plate 53* is one of the best known of these early wall paintings, dating to about AD 500. It illustrates a *jātaka*, or event in one of the past lives of the Buddha. Such stories were an essential part of mahāyāna doctrine aimed at a simple lay public. It tells the story of Brahmadatta, a King of Benares, who was extremely fond of hunting. He threatened to punish anybody who let any deer escape during the hunt and his beaters decided to drive all the beasts towards the king, thus letting him take the responsibility for any which escaped. A stag was driven to the king who shot at it and missed. The stag went past and, taunted by the jeers of his companions, the king pursued it headlong into the forest. There the stag avoided a huge pit half full of water, but the king plunged straight into it and was in danger of drowning. The stag seeing his plight, bore him no malice, but immediately rescued him, set him on his back and returned with him setting him down near his army. The stag refused all rewards and only asked that in return the king observe the good law. A little later the Buddha, to test the king's gratitude and resolve, placed a stag between him and a target at which he was aiming. The king lowered his bow and, ignoring all threats and temptations, put to him by the Buddha in disguise, steadfastly refused to shoot the animal. Sākyamuni then revealed himself to the king and, by way of congratulation, exhorted him to constant vigilance.*

E. B. Cowell and
W. H. D. Rouse: *The Jataka.*
Cambridge, 1901. Vol. IV,
pp. 169–174.

In *plate 53* we see a stylized landscape in which the stag appears frequently as the principal figure in the composition. In the centre, on a slope, the grateful king of Benares kneels to thank his saviour, to the left of this the animal is carrying the king back to his army. The story thus proceeds from right to left in a manner typical of all later narrative painting. Above and to the right the stag is shown lying down. In the story, when the king aimed his arrow, the stag avoided it by rolling over, and the king, thinking that he had wounded the animal, rushed off in pursuit.

Plates 54 and 55 also illustrate jātaka stories. That in *plate 54* is perhaps the most famous of all and tells how the Buddha in a former life, out of compassion for all living creatures, gave his life to feed a starving tigress and her cubs. In the bottom register he is revealed enthroned as the Buddha with two worshippers before him. The landscape is more developed than in the earlier jātaka illustration and the composition more involved.

We know that T'an-yao, who was responsible for starting the Yün-kang caves, was also a considerable translator of the sūtras and among his works was one of AD 476, the *Tsa-pao-tsang-ching,* a collection of stories intended to encourage the reader in his religious faith.* The lay worshippers would immediately recognize such scenes amidst much that must have seemed either esoteric or somewhat repetitive. One must always remember that the artists were simple men working for an unsophisticated public.

S. Mizuno and T. Nagahiro:
Yün-kang. Kyoto, 1954.
Vols. XIII–XIV, p. 95.

One of the main interests in these paintings is the representation of landscape, if indeed one can call these rows of various coloured peaks a true 'landscape'. Hitherto, lack of adequate reproductions has hindered our appreciation of the large part that Tun-huang must play in any account of early Chinese painting. Recent publications, both Chinese and Western, show the skill and imagination of the artists in this outpost of China. What is perhaps more interesting is the stimulus that Buddhist lore, steeped in references to landscape, gave to a people already acutely conscious of the natural world around them.

To the same cave (CCLVII) and period belongs a frieze of the Seven Buddhas of the Past. The whole frieze starts with an enthroned Sākyamuni, then comes a Buddha riding on elephants, another on white horses, and one on animals, interpreted by

Plates 63, 64

Gray, op. cit., p. 39.

C. F. H. Sickman and A. Soper: *The Art and Architecture of China*, pl. 16a, 17a, b, 18.

O. Siren: 'Indian and Other Influences in Chinese Sculpture', in *Studies in Chinese Art and some Indian Influences*. London, 1938. Sickman, op. cit., p. 29.

Gray as monkeys.* However, they are probably lions or the chimera-like animals which appear in Chinese sculpture from the 2nd century onwards.* This beast probably originated in Mesopotamian art, came through Babylon and Assyria to Achaemenid Persia and then through Bactria and across Central Asia to China.*

Even in sculpture the Chinese gave these animals a most powerful body and a plunging sense of rapid movement. The thick neck, swelling chest, heavy jaw and lithe movement are more effectively rendered in painting than in stone. The beard, tail, and horns suggest that the artist may have wished to represent chimeras as far as he understood them. By comparison with the dainty prancing movement of the white horses, they create a tremendous impression of heavy power. The silhouettes of mountains below them effectively convey the sense of height. Above them are five rows of eighteen Buddhas which form part of the Thousand Buddhas in this cave. One finds somewhat similar lions on the arch-ends of Yün-kang caves and these with their heavy open jaws resemble paintings in Shotorak, Afghanistan.

The Seven Buddhas of the Past, the Buddhas in human form, are certainly intended to represent Vipaśyin, the enlightener of the cosmic eon, twice removed from our own, Sikhin, Viśabhū, the teachers of the cosmic eon, immediately previous to our own, Krakucchanda, Kanakamuni, Kaśyapa and Sākyamuni, the renewers of the law for our present world period. However, there are here eight in all and the enthroned Buddha may be intended to represent Maitreya, the Buddha of the future. A sūtra translated by T'an-yao refers to the Seven Buddhas of the Past together with Maitreya being in the Tusita Heaven surrounded by worshippers, and enumerates their supernatural powers and the benefits they can bestow.

O. Siren, op. cit., p. 65.

Contours within the mountains are indicated by additional lines, and vegetation is indicated by large flowers growing above them from the valleys formed by the peaks. There is no doubt that Chinese artists learned a great deal from the Buddhist art centres in Central Asia, but to claim that 'they had evidently not received their fundamental training in China, but further west, at the art centres then existing at Turfan, Kutcha, Khotan and other places along the western routes'* is perhaps to credit Central Asia with too much influence in respect to landscape. Han dynasty bricks and tiles from Szechwan tombs, incidentally quite close geographically to Tun-huang, show landscapes with similar mountain scenes even to the disproportionate foliage springing from the valleys. Some even have hunting scenes with deer

R. C. Rudolph: *Han Tomb Art of West China*. Berkeley and Los Angeles, 1951, pls. 91, 92.

on the mountain sides. These early scenes on brick are in some respects more advanced from a point of view of landscape compositions than the early Tun-huang paintings.* Allowing for the difficulty of representing landscape on stamped brick it is certain that landscape painters, as early as the Han dynasty, some four hundred years before the Wei caves of Tun-huang, had mastered a considerable degree of landscape painting. A similar form for mountains is found in tombs in Manchuria, which Japanese date to the mid-5th century. These contain no Buddhist elements but clearly continue Han traditions.* Here the sense of movement is more vital than in the Wei caves, though the colouring is less pleasant. The only additions from the Buddhist art of Central Asia and India to landscape painting were a vastly expanded repertoire of stories with landscape backgrounds which inspired the imagination of the artists, an urge to narrative compositions which could depict them and a new and more attractive palette. The Chinese artists were quite familiar with the landscape symbols to express these new ideas. They simply injected new life into one of China's oldest pictorial traditions.

H. Ikeuchi, S. Umehara: *T'ung-kou*. Vol. II, pl. XI.

Although much of the strength of the earlier colours has now faded or changed, the effect of these paintings on a worshipper must originally have been brilliant. *Plate 48* shows part of a back wall and ceiling and gives some idea of the effect of a whole cave. Rows of donors occupy the bottom register followed by a broad band with the main scenes—here a seated and a standing Buddha both in the mudrā which banishes fear. They are flanked by disciples while celestials fly in aerial abandon. Above this band come five rows of the Thousand Buddhas and another Buddha group occupies the triangular gable end. A very ornate ceiling imitates a textile canopy, and where flat, it is painted to simulate a coffered beam construction.

The asymmetrical arrangement and the variety of pose and gesture give the figures interest and life. The detail from the central band in *plate 52* shows how the painters, inspired by Central Asian practice, gave the bodies and faces a stylized form of shading which increases the plastic effect of muscles and features. Impressive as the faces may now appear with their exaggerated highlights producing a mask-like effect, much of this bizarre quality is fortuitous and due to the oxidization of the white lead paint used as undercoating for the flesh colours. These, like the outlines, have darkened. The original appearance must have been far more naturalistic and the whole effect more brightly coloured than at present. Altogether the paintings are more warm, varied and animated than the stone carvings of the period at other sites. The gentle rhythms of the long line of disciples are expressed by a vigorous modelling in a few bold lines. No stiff or harsh brush stroke interrupts their languorous sway. The artists obviously did them quickly, but with a considerable mastery of the mediums at their command. It is inspired folk art on a grand scale.

The question arises as to how far the workmanship of Tun-huang is provincial and therefore inferior by comparison with what was being produced in the centres of metropolitan China. Any true assessment of their standard is made difficult by the absence of comparative material. All the wall paintings in temples of the main artistic centres were destroyed in the great Buddhist persecutions of A D 834–835 and by troubles in subsequent centuries. One of the few main sources of comparison are the wall paintings of the Kondō in the Hōryū-ji, Nara, Japan, destroyed by fire in 1949. These were done about A D 700, and according to various scholars, either by Koreans, by Chinese or by Japanese working under Chinese masters. Central Asian influences are strong there, but the various elements of Central Asia and China are much more skilfully combined. Elements of chiaroscuro are still used, but the drawing is more delicate, the faces more refined and personalized, the colours more subtle and the compositions more simple and assured than anything we find on the walls of Tun-huang. The riot of colour is calmed. However, these belong to a period some two hundred years later than the Wei cave paintings, and could only be compared with 7th-century metropolitan Chinese work, if such existed. Popular Japanese Buddhist art as illustrated by 8th-century Japanese illustrated sūtras shows much more affinity with the art of the Wei caves in its treatment of figures, landscape and space. Gray concludes that 'Tun-huang could not have originated any style, and it is evident that, whereas in the Wei dynasty caves, the style was abreast of the most modern China, by later T'ang, Tun-huang can only be regarded as provincial and old-fashioned. At all times, the wall paintings there are to be seen as the work of

B. Gray, op. cit., p. 33.

more or less accomplished artisans, professional painters, but not artists'.* However, the T'ang guardian figures at Tun-huang, judging by what the Japanese copied from metropolitan China, must have been fully comparable to the best produced anywhere. The tradition of landscape painting was continued by the so-called 'northern school' of landscape painting in the T'ang dynasty and is seen in early Yamato-e style painting in Japan. From what we know of both of these, the Tun-huang wall paintings are indeed but provincial reflections of a great art.

The religious art of Tun-huang is intimate. It lacks the grandeur of Yün-kang and Lung-mên; its language is that of popular devotional art as still seen in parts of Europe on a popular local saint's feast-day. Much of it is monotonous and repetitive, but in a surprisingly large number of places are passages of skilled draughtsmanship, radiant colour and vehement faith. If *naïveté* of inspiration and simplicity of vision could produce an art of such sublimated sensuality in the deserts of Kansu, how splendid must have been the now lost masterpieces of central China!

Notes on the plates on page 159

52

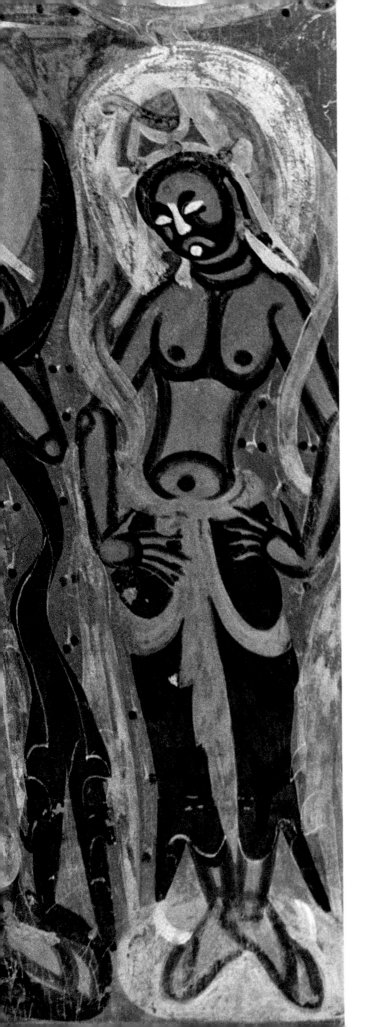

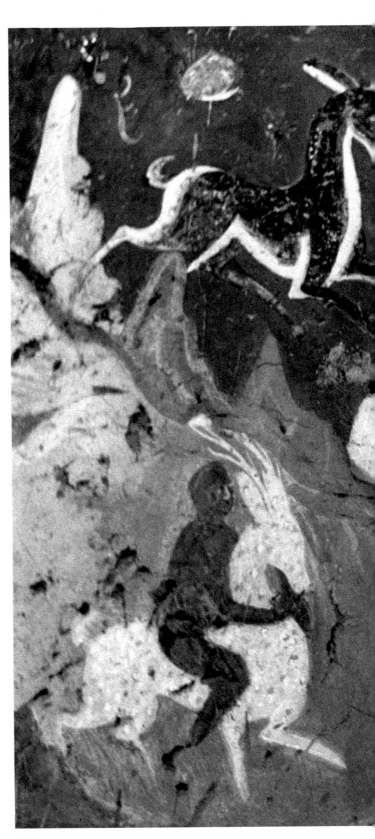

53

54

55

58

59

62

64

NOTES ON THE PLATES TO CHAPTER V

47   WALL PAINTING of Buddha and his acolytes standing on the Vulture Peak, Cave CCLVII, c. AD 500.

48   ONE OF THE WALLS and part of the ceiling of Cave CDXXVIII, early 6th century. See *p. 137*.

49   AMITĀBHA Buddha in the Western Paradise—a fresco in Cave CCXVII, mid-7th century.

50   ONE OF THE SEVEN BUDDHAS of the East—detail of a fresco in Cave DXXVII, c. AD 500.

51   CAVE CCXLIX with its central pillar on which is a Buddha trinity, early 6th century.

52   DETAIL from *plate 48*.

53   DETAIL from a wall painting in Cave CCLVII illustrating the jātaka of the deer, c. AD 500. See *pp. 134/135*.

54   DETAIL from a wall painting in Cave CDXXVIII illustrating the jātaka of Buddha offering himself as food out of compassion for a starving tigress and her young, c. AD 520–530. See *p. 135*.

55   JĀTAKA DETAIL, from the same cave. See *p. 135*.

56   BUDDHA REPELLING Mara's attack, the same cave.

57   HEAD OF A LOHAN in painted clay, detail of *plate 59*. See *p. 132*.

58   HEAD OF A LOHAN in painted clay, detail of *plate 59*. See *p. 132*.

59   BUDDHA AND ATTENDANTS in painted clay, in an unidentified cave, early 7th century. See *p. 132*.

60   ATTENDANT IN PAINTED CLAY, in an unidentified cave, early 7th century.

61   BODHISATTVA in painted clay, Cave CDXXVII, early 7th century. See *p. 130*.

62   SĀKYAMUNI BUDDHA and two bodhisattvas in painted clay, the central trinity in the same cave. See *p. 130*.

63/4 TWO OF THE SEVEN BUDDHAS of the Past—frescoes in Cave CCLVII, c. AD 500. See *p. 136*.

65   THE THOUSAND BUDDHAS. The left-hand part of the trinity in *plate 62*. See *p. 130*.

66   THE THOUSAND BUDDHAS. The trinity to the left of the same cave. See *pp. 130, 133*.

67   FROM LEFT TO RIGHT, lohan, bodhisattva, and lokapāla in painted clay ranged to the Buddha's left in Cave CXCVI, 8th century. See *pp. 130, 132*.

68   PAINTED CLAY LOKAPĀLA in the same cave. See *p. 130*.

69   SEATED BUDDHA, lohans and bodhisattvas in painted clay, a group in the same cave. See *p. 131*.

VI MAI-CHI-SHAN

The only publication in English is a short report with 6 photographs by William Willetts in *Illustrated London News.* February 13, 1954, pp. 236–7.

THE CAVE temples of Mai-chi-shan lie to the east of the ancient Buddhist centre of Liang-chou, some 28 miles southeast of T'ien-shui in Kansu. The mountain into which they are cut belongs to the Ch'in-ling range and derives its name 'Mai-chi' from its shape which resembles sheaves of standing grain. It is a magnificent site with numerous caves cut into its precipitous sides. Strangely enough, due to its remoteness, it had completely escaped the attention of scholars until a group under the direction of Chang Shu-hung, the Director of the Tun-huang Institute, spent just over a month there in 1953. A preliminary survey recorded 194 caves.* A valuable Chinese source work, *Biographies of Eminent Monks,* tells that Mai-chi-shan was a holy site as early as the beginning of the 5th century, and in AD 949 a traveller to the place wrote: 'Up in the blue sky, in the steep rock cliff, the stone is carved to represent Buddha figures. A thousand niches, although fashioned by human effort, are mistakenly thought to be divine workmanship.'

Plates 70, 71 and 72 give an idea of what so impressed this visitor of nearly a thousand years ago. It requires little imagination to appreciate the labour and even the dangers involved in carrying out such a giant enterprise. The results of the centuries of work here are perhaps even more dramatic than at Yün-kang, Lung-mên and Tun-huang. But here too, as at Tun-huang, the rock is of conglomerate type and unsuited to sculpture. Consequently most of the figures were modelled in clay over rough stone or wooden cores. *Plate 82* shows how wooden armatures were sometimes inserted into the walls in order to build up such sharply projecting parts as arms. A *Plate 80* few were carved in stone. The caves date from the Northern Wei period to about AD 1000, and much restoration work was done from that time onwards.

Plates 71, 86 The largest cave is Cave IV or the Upper Ch'i-fo-ko, 'Cave of the Seven Buddhas'. It dominates the eastern cliff and in earlier times a huge wooden outbuilding protected it. This has long since collapsed, but the rows of holes which held the beams for this structure are clearly visible above the niche. A representation in rock of a roof of tiled type once spanned the whole niche, but most of this eroded and collapsed from exposure to the elements when the wooden outbuilding no longer protected it. However, parts of the tiled area and the decorations at each end of the ridge have survived.

The cave consists of seven large niches. On the back of each is a large central Buddha with a pair of figures on each side. Both side walls contain three figures so that the caves each have a total of ten figures. At each end of the outer wall is a large octagonal pillar. The entrances, now much eroded, are basically square with imitations in modelling of curtains and canopies. The niches are very close together, but there is just room between each for a fierce guardian figure.

Plates 101, 102

A valuable source for the dating of these seven niches is the *Ch'in-chou T'ien-shui-chün Mai-chi-shan Fo-k'an*, 'The Buddhist caves of Mai-chi-shan in T'ien-shui Commandery, Ch'in-chou,' by a Northern Ch'i dynasty writer named Yü Hsin which is quoted in his collected works. According to this writer a certain Li Yün-hsin, the governor of Ch'in-chou, ordered seven niches to be carved for the benefit of his father. These are probably the seven niches to which he refers and they must have been made in the years AD 566–568.

The Northern Ch'i dynasty (550–577) and its contemporaneous Northern Chou (557–580) enable us to fill out the political period between the final disintegration of the Northern Wei power and the unification of the country under the Sui dynasty in 589. As a unified political force the Northern Wei had been impotent since about 530. However, Buddhism itself was still a very potent force and we learn for instance that in 533 Hsiao Wu, ruler of the Wei, issued a second edition of the great collection of Buddhist writings known as the Tripitaka. Bodhidarma, perhaps the most famous of all foreign monks, lived at Lo-yang between 516 and 534. To him is credited the founding of the *Ch'an* sect, known in Japanese as *Zen,* a form of Buddhism which was to have a deep and lasting influence on Eastern thought and art. The 6th century saw many innovations in Chinese Buddhism and produced some of the most beautiful of all Buddhist sculpture.

The Northern Wei dynasty itself disappeared in a confusion of internal revolt, which is typical of the end of all great dynasties. It split into an Eastern and Western Wei Empire, but both were ephemeral and were followed by the only slightly more stable Northern Ch'i and Northern Chou. The Northern Ch'i controlled most of the important cave-temple sites and officially adopted the Buddhist faith. The Northern Chou was paramount in the west, away from the main Chinese centres of culture and initiated a persecution of Buddhism.

The works of the Cave of the Seven Buddhas illustrate a most important transitional phase in the history of Chinese Buddhist sculpture between the early art of Yün-kang and Lung-mên and the full Sui-T'ang modelling styles. The change from the stiff hieratical style of the full Northern Wei period to these naturalistic representations marks a complete break with accepted sculptural standards seen at their most developed in the highly spiritualized statues of Lung-mên. In these the heavy drapery was arranged schematically and rhythmically over the flat body which artists never interpreted in human terms. The Mai-chi-shan sculptures are significant in so far as we can see how this early impassivity of face and figure steadily broke down, its place to be taken by new concepts which revolutionized Chinese sculpture. In *plate 97* the folds over the pedestal are beginning to relax. The two halves of the robe are skilfully contrasted and the foot which emerges is no longer as in earlier times, flatly and schematically represented. It is a human foot carved in the round with shapely ankle and naturalistic toes. The two standing figures in *plates 77 and 78* show the next step in the development in which the drapery becomes far more naturalistic, hanging with easy if heavy grace on slender human frames. The body begins to appear beneath the robes. In *plate 79*, although the chest is flat, the stomach swells where it is drawn in by a tight belt and the gentle roundness of the abdomen is emphasized by curved incised lines which follow the contours of the bulge.

The faces share in the re-humanizing process. Modest maidens begin to take the place of the sexless, aloof divinities and attendants. For the first time we see everyday figures elevated to the ranks of religious statuary. The archaic smile ends in what one feels are almost dimples. Such figures come as a surprise and a relief after the rigid formulae of about AD 500 which *en masse* tend to weary the imagination. The figures in *plates 75, 79 and 91*, some of the most attractive of the whole site, are simply dressed with hair discreetly tied and surmounted by a flower. The neck-plate, a basic decoration on Buddhist attendants, is flat and undecorated. The sculptors have not yet succumbed to the temptation to load their figures with heavy and ornate jewellery. The eyes have a frank and worldly look. Fortunately the heads of these figures have escaped restoration.

The custom of restoring statues throughout the centuries according to the fortunes of Buddhism adds greatly to the historian's problems. In stone sculpture one can, of course, distinguish restorations with relative ease, but this is not so with clay statues where it is easy to apply a new coat of clay and then repaint the whole area. Such repairs were often carried out at successive periods over as much as a thousand years or more.

The T'ien Wang, or Heavenly King, in Cave XLIII is one of the Guardians of the *Plate 103* Four Cardinal Directions, or one of a pair of similar kings usually set up as guardians of a temple gate. It was made during the T'ang dynasty but remodelled during the Sung period—as were also the companion figures in *plates 98 and 99*. The figure in *plate 100*, dating to the Sui period, shows the appearance of such a guardian figure before the Sung restoration. The head in *plate 91* is a mid-6th-century head, but faithfully repaired in later centuries. The figures in the niches of the Cave of the Seven *Plate 101* Buddhas were repainted and restored in the Ming (1368-1644) and the Ch'ing dynasties (1644-1911). The mid-6th-century guardians on the fronts of the niches of *Plate 102* the Seven Buddhas were remodelled in the T'ang period, and here in places the two layers of clay can easily be distinguished. It is easy to recognize the relationship between these guardian figures and those at Lung-mên. With their exaggerated *Plate 41* gestures and grimacing faces they breathe the martial vigour of the full T'ang period.

So also these figures begin to free themselves from the rock in which they were carved. Most of the early figures remain entrapped in the stone or closely attached *Plates 76–78* to it. The T'ang dynasty inherited the developments of sculpture in the round made in the 6th century.

Just as the sculptures of Mai-chi-shan span the transitional years between the end of Wei and the beginning of Sui-T'ang art, so also they lead us from the end of the T'ang into the Sung dynasty (960-1276).

The official date for the end of the T'ang is given as 907, but the dynasty in fact really came to an end when its brilliant capital at Ch'ang-an was sacked by a rebellious army in 881. From that time the nominal T'ang emperor was in the hands of a warlord who finally forced him to abdicate in 907. This was the culmination of a process which had gathered strength from the time of An Lu-shan's rebellion in 755. From that time the power of the central administration, the basis of T'ang rule, lacked the strength effectively to guard against external attack or to curb the grow- C. P. Fitzgerald: *China*. ing independence of local governors.* London 1935.

The fifty-three years following the end of T'ang are known as the Five Dynasties period. It was one of political chaos and civil war in which each of these so-called dynasties was little more than a military dictatorship which seized as much of the country as it could. The longest lasted seventeen years, the shortest only ten. Other states in the south and west preserved their independence and continued the traditions of Chinese culture relatively untroubled.

In the Sung dynasty we witness the rare phenomenon in Chinese history of an age which was truly and fundamentally pacifist. The country was weary of war and unsettled times. Most intelligent and educated men in the troubled Five Dynasties period had avoided public service even though it was their main source of livelihood. Its rewards were no recompense for the dangers inherent in service to unscrupulous military opportunists. But the traditions of Chinese culture were strong. China knew it must be a united country and the man the army made the first emperor of the Sung was sufficiently strong and respected to persuade those who had put him on the throne at the point of a sword to lay down those same swords and disband their armies. They trusted him to respect their confidence and he did not betray them. However, the seeds were sown which were to contribute much to the weakening and eventual overthrow of the dynasty. The barbarians in the north had secured a strong foothold south of the Great Wall. They occupied what is now Peking and they were only kept at bay by the temporary means of bribery. Western Kansu was also independent of Sung rule so that China did not control the routes into Central Asia and to India. This had cultural and artistic repercussions.

The pacifist tenor of the Sung centuries favoured the arts, which flourished to a degree unknown previously. The painting and ceramics of the Sung are generally reckoned to be the finest flowers of all Chinese art. This was an age of learning and culture which infused the whole life of the time. The invention of printing made scholarship more widely diffused than ever before and knowledge of China's past literature became the criterion for success in the civil service examinations. Philosophic controversy was the main intellectual activity. Confucianism saw its heyday, but Confucius himself would have been most surprised by its new form. It no longer excluded Buddhist ways of thought for Buddhism had penetrated so deeply into the Chinese mind that Confucian thinkers incorporated much of it into their new interpretations of the ideal way of life taught by the Sage. The same was true of Taoism. This, in fact, was one of the few periods in which the rulers tried, according to their interpretations, to put the teachings of Confucius into practice. The introspection which Buddhism encouraged was a feature of Sung civilization and finds its reflection as much in a landscape as in a flower-shaped bowl. The violent passions which Buddhism had once inspired in Confucians died when the Confucians were in undisputed authority. And it was a Buddhism which was now completely Chinese. In India Buddhism was being exterminated by the Muslim invasions to such a degree that it disappeared in the very country of its origin. The vital road to the west was blocked and the two-way stream of religious men ceased. China was thus thrust back on itself for new developments in the Buddhist faith. Of these, by far the most vital was that of the Ch'an or Zen (Japanese) sect.

The majority of our knowledge of Sung dynasty sculpture is derived from the graceful wooden Kuan-yins, examples of which are found in most Western museums. In these plump full figures, human characteristics are more insistent than in even the T'ang figures. They generally sit in that ultimate of relaxed poses, the *maharaja-lila,* or position of royal ease. Elegant flowing drapery surrounds mature female figures which are far removed from the ideal of the bodhisattva, the saint who has gone beyond all that is worldly. They are, as Grousset described them, more like a bejewelled and rather ripe prima donna with the majestic indolence of a sultana. The carving seems to defy the material from which they are made. This is the model which in later times, and always following the fashion of feminine beauty of the day, inspired the elegant *blanc-de-chine* figures of the Ming and Ch'ing periods.

The Mai-chi-shan caves also contain some remarkable monumental Sung figures which come close to portraiture. The bodhisattvas and donors in Cave CLXV wear over their ample figures robes of discreetly cut and heavy cloth. Here, one feels, is an affected simplicity in which the rich texture of the cloth is cleverly suggested by the way the material hangs. The well-fed smooth faces and the well-groomed coiffures combine to represent an aristocracy which is of this world rather than the next. The patrons of the church now obviously expected to find themselves in effigy before the works which they patronized. The energy of the T'ang has dissolved into a refined complacency. One feels that this is the triumph of fashion over faith.

Plates 104, 106, 107

The same cannot be said of the superb head of a monk in *plate 108*. A number of large glazed portrait figures of monks have survived from the north where Sung domain did not reach but where Buddhism flourished. In Japan, too, such figures inspired the famous Muchaku and Seshin of the Kōfuku-ji of 1208. This Mai-chi-shan monk is also probably intended to represent an Indian priest and, though an imaginary portrait, it carries naturalism in sculpture to a degree unknown in previous times.

The Sung guardians betray a similar intoxication with surfaces. Their exaggerated muscles and outstanding veins and, what is new in Chinese sculpture, a tremendous sense of movement in free standing figures created a new form which was taken up with enthusiasm, especially in Japan. The energy they exude is superhuman, their faces terrifying masks which set off the passivity of the other divinities. Of all Chinese sculpture they come nearest to some Western nude studies and show how far the Chinese could reach without a profound study of anatomy. In abandoning their search for spirituality and beginning an interest in naturalistic face and form the Chinese were opening a completely new approach to sculpture which they were unwilling to follow to its logical conclusions. They covered their lack of knowledge by an increasing technical mastery in the depiction of drapery—a branch of sculpture in which they are unsurpassed.

Notes on the plates on pages 195/196

73

74

79

80

83

84

87

90

89

88

91

92

93

96

94

97

95

99

NOTES ON THE PLATES TO CHAPTER VI

70 PART OF THE CLIFF FACE of Mai-chi-shan showing at top right, part of the trinity of Cave XIII, probably of Sui dynasty date (589–618). See *p. 160.*

71 GENERAL VIEW of the main caves of Mai-chi-shan. See *p. 160.*

72 THE GALLERY of the Thousand Buddhas, Cave III, early 6th century. See *p. 160.*

73 CAVE CXCI. Buddha and bodhisattvas seated on lotuses, probably of the Sung dynasty (960–1279).

74 PROFILE OF THE CENTRAL BUDDHA in Cave XIII (probably 589–618).

75 LEFT-HAND ATTENDANT, clay, Cave LX (*c.* 535—556 with later restorations).

76 UPPER TWO ROWS of the Thousand Buddhas in Cave III, stone with clay restorations, early 6th century. See *p. 163.*

77 CLAY KUAN-YIN on the right-hand wall of Cave C (490–500). See *pp. 162/163.*

78 CLAY ATTENDANT to the right of the central figure in Cave LX (535–556). See *pp. 162/163.*

79 ATTENDANT. See *p. 162.*

80 BODHISATTVA in an unidentified cave (535–556). See *p. 163.*

81 PAINTED CLAY KUAN-YIN in Cave LXIX (after AD 500).

82 CLAY FIGURE of the 6th century extensively restored under the Ming dynasty (14th–17th centuries). See *p. 160.*

83/4 BUDDHA in passage to Nirvāṇa, clay, Cave I, 6th century, with extensive Ming dynasty restoration.

85 SEATED BUDDHA in clay in the right-hand wall of Cave CXXIII (535–556).

86 GENERAL VIEW of Cave IV ('The Cave of the Seven-Buddha Niches') along its façade gallery, basically Northern Wei (385–535) but with T'ang (618–906) and Sung (960–1279) restorations. See *p. 160.*

87 CLAY SEATED BUDDHA in an unidentified cave, first quarter of the 6th century.

88 CLAY SEATED BUDDHA.

89 GUARDIAN KING on the gallery in front of Cave V, basically early 6th century, but extensively restored in the Sung period (960–1279).

90 CLAY HEAD of a bodhisattva or attendant in an unidentified cave (535–556).

91 CLAY HEAD of an attendant on the left-hand wall of Cave L (535–556 with later restorations). See *pp. 162/163.*

92 CLAY HEAD of a seated Buddha on the left-hand wall of Cave LXII (589–618).

93 CLAY HEAD of a Buddha in an unidentified cave, Sui dynasty (589–618) with Sung dynasty (960–1279) restorations.

94 CLAY HEAD of a standing Buddha in Cave CXIII, T'ang dynasty (618–906) with extensive restorations later.

95 CLAY HEAD of a seated Buddha in Cave CXXVII (?), early 6th century with extensive Sung (906–1279) restorations.

96 PART OF THE FRIEZE of the Thousand Buddhas in Cave III (?), early 6th century, the heads restored.

97 TYPICAL DRAPERY over the pedestal of a seated Buddha of c. 535–556. See *p. 162*.

98 A GATE GUARDIAN at the left end of the gallery outside Cave IV ('The Cave of the Seven-Buddha Niches'); see *plate 86*. A mid-6th-century original with extensive Sung (960–1279) restorations. See *p. 163*.

99 ANOTHER GATE GUARDIAN at the left end of the same gallery. Mid-6th-century original with Sung restorations. See *p. 163*.

100 CLAY HEAD of a guardian figure in Cave XIV, the unrestored Sui dynasty (589–618) style. See *p. 163*.

101 PART OF THE FAÇADE of Cave IV, 'The Cave of the Seven-Buddha Niches', showing the entrance to one of these niches with a bodhisattva in view restored in the Ming period (1368–1644), and one of the guardians in relief that come between the niches, restored under the T'ang (618–907). See *pp. 161, 163*.

102 DETAIL OF THE CLAY RELIEF GUARDIAN between niches two and three in Cave IV, also restored under the T'ang. See *pp. 162/163*.

103 DETAIL OF A GUARDIAN in clay, Cave XLIII, extensively restored under the Sung (960–1279). See *p. 163*.

104 THE CLAY ATTENDANTS flanking the main Kuan-yin figure (*plate 106*) in Cave CLXV, Sung dynasty (960–1279). See *p. 165*.

105 CLAY FIGURE of the disciple Kasyāpa, Cave LXXXVII (c. 520–530).

106 CLAY FIGURE of Kuan-yin, the central figure of Cave CLXV, Sung dynasty (960–1279). See *p. 165*.

107 DETAIL OF THE CLAY ATTENDANT to the left of the Kuan-yin in Cave CLXV, Sung dynasty (960–1279). See *plate 104*, and *p. 165*.

108 CLAY LOHAN, possibly Kasyāpa, in Cave XC, extensively restored under the Sung (960–1279). See *p. 165*.

VII CERAMICS AND PAINTING

In a general context of Chinese art ceramics and painting must be taken as playing two of the most important roles, but here, in a book on the monumental art of China, their roles are much more limited. Neither are monumental by nature, but it can be said that both have at certain times formed an accompaniment to or have even been given the treatment of monumental art.

In ceramic art the pottery figures of the Han and the T'ang dynasties in particular show a similar development towards naturalism as does the sculpture of the cave temples, but in an even freer manner. They represent the secular side of Chinese figurative art while being of religious import to the extent that they were made for burial in the tombs of the well-to-do. Painting in its earlier stages of development had an even closer association with the art of the cave temples. The wall paintings at Tun-huang are the largest and almost the only group of T'ang and pre-T'ang paintings available to us and they provide us with some early examples of the landscape painting to which the Chinese were later to devote so much of their attention. Only in this special field, landscape painting, can Chinese painting be said to have had a sense of monumentality, and then only in the awesome landscapes of the Five *Plate 118* Dynasties and early Sung periods to be described later.

From very early times in the development of their civilization, that is to say from about the 3rd millennium B C, the Chinese have shown innate skill in the ceramic arts. Even their neolithic pottery, both in skill of manufacture and assurance of design, surpasses that of any other culture at a similar stage in its development. Again during the Shang dynasty, a little very refined, highly-fired white ware was produced which seem to foreshadow the invention of porcelain by over two thousand years.

The Chinese have continued to lead the world in the development of ceramics and in the T'ang period they were the first people, by some eight hundred years, to discover the secret of the manufacture of pure porcelain. The refined shapes and

197

subtle glazes of the wares of the Sung dynasty give them a strong claim to be considered the finest that the world has seen.

The first real flowering of pottery manufacture took place during the Han dynasty when a wide range of vessels, objects and figures were made for burial with the dead. Many of the pots of this time were made in frank imitation of simple bronzes. The shapes are sturdy in these vases and jars, but more interesting is a whole range of architectural models ranging from many-storied pavilions, complete with their inhabitants, down to tiny chicken runs, from granaries to pig-sties, from large cooking stoves to drinking cups—all intended to serve the after-life of the buried. They furnish a most vivid picture of the life in China some two thousand years ago.

The Chinese discovered glaze some time before the Han dynasty, but they mastered its application during these productive four centuries. The most popular glaze was of a lively green colour produced by a lead glaze, the colour being derived from copper silicates. Burial, or simply age, often produces in these green glazes an iridescence which greatly enhances their appearance, in the same way that a patina enlivens the surface of a bronze. Indeed it makes the pottery look more like bronze. Thus, as wealth and the customs of the nobility spread among the less elevated classes of early Chinese society, far more could aspire at least to the semblance of noble burial—a tendency which had been growing in previous centuries. The vessels of this time are almost always heavily potted, simply designed and unpretentious but of a restrained vigour. Their confidence raises them well above the pedestrian and reflects the assurance of the Chinese world of Han.

A more important ceramic innovation during this period was that of a fine glazed stoneware which came to be known as Yüeh ware from the area in which it was made. Two basic types are recognized—that from the Chiu-yen or 'Nine Rocks' kilns in Chekiang and a more refined variety from Shang-lin Lake in the Yüeh-chou area itself. The latter type very early attracted the admiration of connoisseurs, indeed it may well have been responsible for the beginnings of Chinese connoisseurship in ceramics. Yüeh ware continued in high esteem down to about the 10th century. It has been claimed that the steady refinements made in this ware and then the discovery of white burning *kaolin* clay at a place of that name led to the momentous discovery of pure porcelain in the late 9th century to early 10th century. Certainly Yüeh wares were the forerunners of the later celadons which form a notable proportion of Chinese ceramics.

We have seen that, on the few occasions when they so desired, the Chinese were able to obtain in their modelling a high degree of naturalistic representation.

However, it was not until the Han dynasty that the human figure played any part in art. Then suddenly a whole new world opened to Chinese artists and craftsmen. The figural representations show the beginnings of a command of sculptural techniques, and with the introduction of Buddhist art, as the cave temples show, the art blossomed in an unprecedented way. The noble religious monuments of Buddhism inspired not only the representation of gods and goddesses but also that of priests of the faith and finally the ordinary believers among the people who either gave money to enable the sculptures to be made or who simply appear in the minor roles of worshippers. The personalities of the various disciples were recorded in the scriptures and the Chinese studied how to depict the various types. But religion apart, the ceramic workers, like the painters, were obviously intrigued with the even wider range provided by the secular, everyday world about them. One senses in the humour of even the early figures, a new joy with which a craftsman approached his subject. One finds repetitions, but always one appreciates an absence of mechanical duplication. In Han the magic and mystery of earlier times met the materialism of a new age. The materialism was to conquer.

It is curious that in the period between Han and T'ang, although monumental Buddhist sculpture reached great heights, the tomb figures which have survived are almost invariably rather clumsy. However, with the T'ang dynasty the lessons of Buddhist sculptural techniques were allied to an even greater wealth and intellectual curiosity than during the preceding centuries. In the thousands of T'ang tomb figures which have been preserved, this cosmopolitan period comes vividly to life. And what a period of explosive creativity it was! The modellers were free of the constricting requirements of Buddhist iconography. So dancing girls, actresses, servants, entertainers, dwarfs, negroes, Central Asiatics, Javanese, Indians, Jewish traders— all the colourful throng of the bustling streets of a prosperous Chinese city find a still reflection in the tombs of the wealthy. Ponderous camels, proud horses, heavy bullocks—the animals who brought the riches of the world to Ch'ang-an, servants and attendants, all the 'status symbols' of T'ang life share a silent vigil. The figures range from a few inches to several feet in height and appear either unglazed or in a variety of glazes from green to brown, cream and blue as well as in mottled varieties of all three. Foreign influences from as far west as Sassanian Persia are immediately visible. So great was the temptation to fill the tombs that an Imperial order of 741 restricted the number of objects which might be placed in a single tomb.* One can readily understand how this art dazzled the whole Eastern world and was eagerly copied by aspiring but less wealthy, less cultivated countries like Japan. Movement,

W. B. Honey: *The Ceramic Art of China and Other Countries of the Far East*. London, 1945, p. 42.

modelling, colour—all contribute to the lively naturalism which is the essence of the art of T'ang. The history and literature of the period give additional proof of the maturity of these centuries. A restrained sensuality as seen in the poetry is perhaps the keynote of the arts of the period. There seems no room for gross emotions. Allied with exquisite feeling and workmanship, this produced a sensuous beauty of line, an art of vigour, strength and monumentality.

These tomb figures bring us nearer to the Chinese of the T'ang than at any other period. If a poet speaks of an evening spent with friends, or wine or women we can actually see the cups he drank from and, among the figures, models of the ladies who charmed the night away, their long sleeves swirling in the air as they danced. For idealist or materialist, thinker or adventurer, man of religion or sensualist, the great centuries of the T'ang dynasty must have been one of civilization's most satisfying periods in which to have lived.

We have seen how the murals at Tun-huang provide excellent examples of early wall painting in a provincial site. We know from literary records that the temples of the main cities, especially those of Ch'ang-an, were also decorated with splendid wall paintings, but unfortunately none of these survived the proscriptions of Buddhism—especially that of 845—or the subsequent neglect during the centuries which followed.

Meanwhile artists had also been exploring various secular forms of painting. Non-religious figural subjects have been found on the walls of tombs from a wide area of the Han Empire. Allowing for the unsettled times in the Six Dynasties period, great advances must have been made in secular painting on scrolls—the type of painting for which China is famous. As early as the 5th century AD, Hsieh Ho, the father of Chinese painting theory, drew up what seem even now quite sophisticated rules to guide the aspiring painter. His first and most famous dictum enjoined an artist to seek to reflect the life-breath and create a sense of movement. It has guided almost every Chinese painter since his day.

From the comparatively little that has survived, one can see that the T'ang enjoyed as brilliant a development in all types of painting as it did in the other arts. Imperial patronage encouraged painters on a hitherto unprecedented scale. New subjects became accepted into the artists' repertoires. Fairy stories, portraits, illustrations of moral precepts, court scenes showing ladies at work or play, spirited horses like those familiar from tomb figures, all reflect aspects of the life of these centuries. In all these works painted in ink and colour on silk or paper an uncompromising naturalism is the artist's aim—deep into the most subtle of all truth-to-life, an inner spirit which creates a sense of movement. They share the quality of full-blooded reality which is characteristic of the T'ang period.

During the T'ang period also the Chinese began the exploration of one of the themes through which their art has made one of its most individual contributions to the artistic vision of the world—pure landscape painting. One can here touch only briefly and in very general terms on a wide subject. The beginnings of interest in landscape can be traced back to the Han and to the backgrounds of religious paintings such as we see at Tun-huang. Thus the beginnings of Chinese landscape painting were very similar to those in the West. What we understand by the T'ang style was the logical successor to these early experiments. It is a highly colourful style of which the best known example is the famous *Emperor Ming Huang's Journey to Szechwan* *Plate 117* attributed to one of the great names of early landscape painting, Li Ssû-hsün (7th to 8th centuries), but possibly a faithful 11th-century copy. In this the landscape features are highly formalized and act like an impressive stage setting to the horses and figures who weave their way through the coulisses. The conventions created during these centuries for expressing rocks and clouds find constant repetition throughout Chinese painting, and the Japanese, who were dazzled by and strove to emulate Chinese civilization at this period, adopted it and made it into one of their national styles. Strangely enough the Chinese later scorned this colourful naturalism as being the hall-mark of the 'professional' landscape painter and motivated by impure sentiments.

The second basic style in Chinese landscape painting depends less on colour and naturalism and more on ink and the brushwork which comes from a long training in the allied art of calligraphy. It seeks the essentials, dwells on outlines and, leaving much to the imagination, stimulates rather than flatters, evokes rather than records. This, too, had its origins in the T'ang dynasty, according to tradition at the brush of Wang Wei (699–759) whom the later scholar-critics praise for his other-worldly, disinterested cultivation of the arts. He became the model scholar-civil-servant, poet, musician and painter—the complete man.

The short period following the fall of T'ang, the so-called Five Dynasties period, was a dangerous half-century for the scholar-administrators. Many of them sought refuge by living like hermits in the depths of the country. This enforced exile from the cities and the realization that, in a changing world, only nature remains immutable created a new vision of landscape as noble, overwhelming and awesome. Man is insignificant—his stature that of an ant among the rocks and quite powerless in face of the huge forces of nature. This respectful attitude continued for a while *Plate 118* when peace and settled conditions returned under the Sung, but during the second half of the Sung period, the luxury and refinement of court life created an atmosphere in which man once more felt himself to be master of the universe. Painters enjoyed court patronage and landscape became a beautiful but tame, somewhat sentimental background to their delicate emotions. The style they created was in itself most affecting—a scholar sits under a tree gazing at the moon, a misty stretch of water or a valley opens before him, a few mountain tops emerge in the shrouded distance. The landscape revolves around himself and his emotions. The brushwork is highly skilled and techniques of expression were studied and evolved. The passages of landscape are invariably lyrical and gently moving, but in such a relaxed atmosphere the emotions can often be rather thin. It is perhaps unfortunate for the reputation of Chinese painting that Western experience of it is largely restricted to later examples in this mood and to decorative flower paintings.

It might be claimed for painters like Huang Kung-wang (1269–1354) and Wang Mêng (1310–1385) of the Yüan dynasty, who retreated to the countryside from public life under the Mongols, that they are true successors of the Five Dynasties masters of the monumental landscape. It is true that they did, as did their masters, paint from direct experience of nature, and certainly they came closer to their ideals than any other painters, but in fact they expressed themselves in new ways and created a different style and set of ideals, themselves becoming the idols of Ming dynasty painters who in turn worked in a far more artificial medium and on a far more personal scale.

Notes on the plates on page 211

110

111

112

113

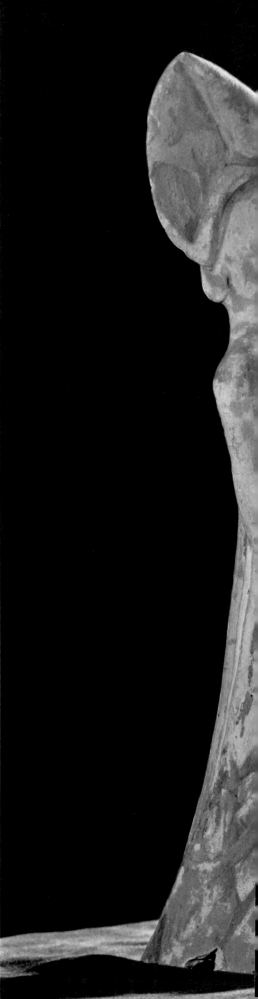

青綠潮山迥
崎嶇道路長
空人多結束行
李自周詳經
為名利郍
舉勞與忙年
陳失姓氏北宋
近乎唐
甲午新秋
尚題

NOTES ON THE PLATES TO CHAPTER VII

109 HORSE AND RIDER—T'ang dynasty (618–907) clay tomb figurine, height 19 cm (7¹/₂″). *Musée Guimet, Paris.*

110 T'ANG DYNASTY clay tomb figurine. *Musée Guimet, Paris.*

111 A FEMALE DANCER—T'ang dynasty clay tomb figurine, 7th century, height 26 cm (10¹/₄″). *Musée Cernuschi, Paris.*

112 A FEMALE DANCER—17th-century clay tomb figurine, height 27 cm. *Musée Cernuschi, Paris.*

113 T'ANG DYNASTY clay tomb figurine, height 24 cm. *Musée Guimet, Paris.*

114 COURT LADY—8th-century clay figurine, height 36 cm (14¹/₈″). *Musée Cernuschi, Paris.*

115 COURT LADY—7th-century clay figurine, height 30 cm (11³/₄″). *Musée Cernuschi, Paris.*

116 COURT LADY—late 6th to early 7th-century clay figurine, height 30 cm. *Musée Cernuschi, Paris.*

117 LANDSCAPE—'Emperor Ming Huang's journey to Szechwan' in ink and colour on paper, attributed to Li Ssû-hsün (651–716), but possibly an 11th-century copy. *National Museum of Formosa. See p. 201.*

118 LANDSCAPE—'Festival for Evoking Rain' in ink and colour on silk, attributed to Tung Yüan (fl. 947–970). *National Museum of Formosa. See pp. 197, 201.*

VIII THE TOMBS OF THE MING EMPERORS

THE ART produced during the Sung centuries ranks among the finest creations of mankind. In their politics the Sung made some interesting experiments in economic policy, but their foreign relations were marked by fundamental weaknesses which led to their destruction. The growing power of the northern tribes beyond the Great Wall had forced the peace-loving, politically inept Sung rulers increasingly to surrender their hold on territory in the north of the country and to retreat to the safer southern areas. Attempts to hold off the northerners by bribery only delayed the inevitable. During the second part of their reign they only controlled half of the country. Finally in the 12th century, Genghiz Khan united the most warlike of all these nomadic tribes, the Mongols, and began his campaign of world conquest across Asia. His grandson, Kublai, crushed any remaining barbarian opposition which stood between him and China and then completely overwhelmed the Chinese Empire. He swept away the Sung dynasty and adopted the Imperial title in 1260. The Mongol, or to give it its Chinese name, the Yüan dynasty, which he established, lasted just over a hundred years and made no contribution whatsoever to the monumental art of China. Only those crafts which could minister to Mongol needs were tolerated.

It was fortunate for Chinese traditions that, after a comparatively short period, the Mongol Empire split up and its leadership disintegrated. The branch which ruled China added to a corrupt administration an economic and political policy which proved suicidal. The despair to which they reduced the Chinese led them to revolt and in 1368 to the Ming restoration.

The Mongol Empire, in its finest hour, stretched over a vast area of the known world from the eastern seaboard of China almost to the heart of Europe. The Mongols thus created the largest land empire the world has ever seen. The trail of destruction left in the wake of their conquests fills another chapter in the long history of these nomadic peoples. It should be pointed out here that in one way or another they contributed more to the world than they are credited with. It is understandable that the historians, and one means in particular the Chinese historians, have been unwilling to credit them with anything positive. In fact it was the Mongols who for the first time brought East and West together in direct contact. Without the *pax tartarica* which their iron rule created across Asia, men like Marco Polo could not have travelled to China.

The Ming dynasty was a restoration in the full sense. It restored a native Chinese to the throne—albeit a man of obscure origins. It restored China's traditional boundaries. It reaffirmed the Chinese belief in their traditional standards. It brought that peace and prosperity which the Chinese consider their birthright, and it returned to them the leadership of East Asia. It subdued for nearly three centuries the barbarian threat in the north and its armies once again controlled the great routes into Central Asia. However, tranquillity was the touchstone of Ming policy and they desperately feared any innovations which might spoil the even tenor of its days. Its ceramics, lacquer, cloisonnée and architecture, though sometimes gaudy, are notable products and in many instances laid the foundation for the technical masterpieces of the 17th and particularly the 18th centuries.

Historians of the great Chinese arts of painting and sculpture have been somewhat critical of the products of the Ming dynasty. Why did Chinese sculpture decline so rapidly from the fall of the Sung onwards? Certainly the tradition had been broken by the devastating Mongol occupation of the country. The population of China had been almost halved and it is unlikely that the financial backing existed to support the vast army of workmen who had laboured on the huge cave projects. It is probable that after a century the workmen themselves no longer existed. It is true that, mainly from fear of anything native Chinese, the Mongols favoured Buddhism, but it was particularly the Tibetan form of Buddhism which received their support and this had no tradition of monumental stone sculpture. Certainly the Confucians were out of favour. Buddhist priests were freed from the restrictions of the law, their temples enriched and exempted from taxes. In time they became another hated instrument in the hands of the oppressors of the Chinese population. The standard of religious feeling seems to have been low, and when the Confucians returned to power under the Ming, they had little difficulty in discrediting their rivals. The civil service which had provided much impetus for Buddhist art in Sung times was at its lowest and most corrupt under the Mongols. Most men of genuine sensitivity and piety retired to the country to avoid the dangers of public service. This may not have injured the painters—indeed it may well have helped them, but it proved unfortunate for sculpture. Hardly a single piece of sculpture exists which we can date to the Yüan dynasty.

Buddhism was dead in the land of its origin, crushed by the Muslim invaders. The Ming armies controlled the Central Asian routes to India, but the inspiration of India had gone and these routes, even for trade, were no longer as important as the new sea routes to the west which the Ming were courageously exploring.

Thus, the Ming had no unbroken sculptural tradition on which to build. Politically they looked back to the great days of the T'ang dynasty when the country was united, powerful and well-administered. Culturally they built on the achievements of the T'ang and Sung. Their sculpture developed along the lines laid down by the Chinese in past centuries, and these pointed towards increased naturalism. The arts, literature and general tenor of the Ming dynasty lead one to suspect that the Ming held no strong opinions about anything, and this spiritual emptiness is sometimes reflected in their arts of painting and sculpture.

The Ming rulers, conscious of their obscure origins, felt obliged to assert themselves. In their art they showed the characteristics typical of *parvenus* and their taste was frankly grandiose.

The first emperor, Hung-wu, of the Ming dynasty, established his capital at Nanking in the south. This was the wise decision of a man of great courage, political acumen and administrative ability. There too he built his palace and reconstructed the city on lines which have survived to this day. Much of what his successors did followed his example. This is particularly true of his tomb in the outskirts of the *Plates 119, 120, 121* city and it is interesting to see how even in the short period of less than thirty years between the building of his tomb and that of his successor, Yung-lo, the power and inspiration had weakened. Here is an object lesson in the difference between an original and a copy. The earlier figures still breathe some of the martial vigour of T'ang times—Yung-lo's figures, in particular those of mythological creatures, are by comparison lifeless and dry.

Perhaps the most far-reaching innovation was the transfer of the capital back to what became known as Peking. The decision of Emperor Yung-lo to leave the economically rich and culturally developed centre of Nanking and return to the comparative poverty of the Peking area was momentous. It involved building a new city. The canal system which brought the wealth of the south to the north in the reverse direction of the flow of the natural waterways had to be repaired and extended. The move back to Peking also involved the reversal of the direction of flow of population which, since T'ang times at least, had been towards the south.

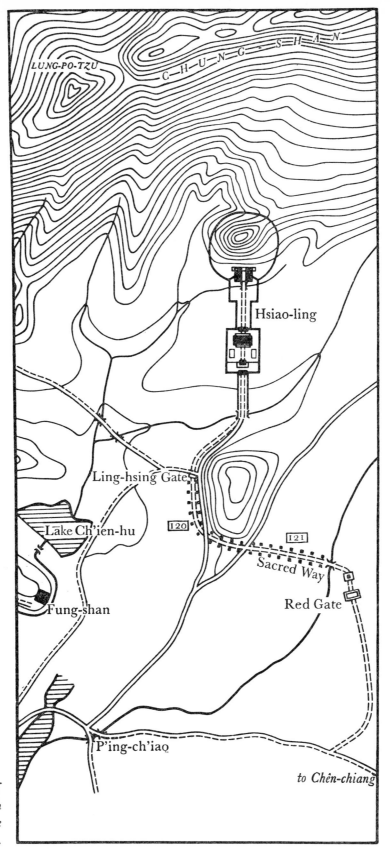

Labels within the map:

LUNG-PO-TZU

C-H-U-N-G—S-H-A-N

Hsiao-ling

Ling-hsing Gate

Lake Ch'ien-hu

120

121

Sacred Way

Fung-shan

Red Gate

P'ing-ch'iao

to Chên-chiang

12   Plan of the tomb of
Hung-wu and the approach
to it, near Nanking. See
plates 120/121.

However, this site close to the Great Wall was strategically better placed for the protection of the empire against the northerners and it was this district that Yung-lo had ruled when he was still a prince and before he seized the throne. Under his building schemes, Peking became one of the finest capitals in the world. Here he gave full license to his *penchant* for the grandiose—large buildings and houses laid out in a most stately scheme intended to attract the new population. We now often see only the large paintings and craft works intended to decorate them and they may seem, out of context, a little pretentious and heavy. But there was some taste and much energy in the people who could conceive Peking and build it into the spacious city it has remained ever since.

After Peking itself the tomb of Emperor Yung-lo is perhaps the most impressive sculptural monument of the Ming period.

Plates 122–125

Yung-lo is the name of the reign period of Emperor Ch'êng-tsu who ruled China 1403–1424. As with subsequent Emperors, he is generally known by his reign name. He was in fact a usurper. The founder of the Ming dynasty had been succeeded by his grandson, but the fourth son of the founder of the dynasty, who was to become Emperor Yung-lo, dethroned him and assumed the title. This act, of course, displeased the scholars who always stressed the importance of legitimacy in matters of succession. His struggle to obtain the throne lasted four years and devasted the heart of China. Nevertheless, he was an able and energetic ruler under whose policy the influence of Ming China reached its greatest extent. He constantly harrassed the barbarians in Mongolia, in the determination to destroy for ever the threat from the north. He personally led five expeditions into Mongolia. He came to terms with the Japanese who were making piratical raids on the coasts of China—a threat later to become very serious. He occupied much of Annam and sent naval expeditions as far as India and Ceylon. Indeed, in historical perspective, these naval expeditions which were able to extract tribute from places as far away as Java and which visited East Africa and the Persian Gulf must rank as one of the period's most notable achievements. In spite of this China was to remain a land empire and never to become a sea power.

His efforts at home were directed towards the rehabilitation of lands laid waste by the wars which brought him to power. Though privately he favoured Buddhism, he officially supported the Confucian scholars on whom the efficient administration of the country depended, and to win them over he encouraged the study of the classics. A typical method of gaining their favour was the launching of the huge literary compilation, the *Yung-lo Ta-tien*, which was to include approximately

23,000 volumes, and thus preserve the best from the sea of Chinese literature. The cost was so enormous that much of the work remained in manuscript.

His reign also marks the beginning of the rise of the eunuch class which was to seize and misuse power. Their evil influence contributed greatly to the fall of the dynasty some three centuries later.

The tomb of the Emperor Yung-lo is at Nan-k'ou, Chih-li, some 25 miles north of Peking. A broad impressive avenue approaching it is lined with monoliths of men and animals carved in blue limestone. Six military officials are dressed in coats of mail reaching down below the knees and wear close-fitting helmets hanging over the shoulders. Some hold swords in the right hand and marshal's batons in the *Plate 122* left. Others have hands clasped on their breasts or lean on swords. The civil officials have robes with long hanging sleeves and tasselled sashes. Some lean on staffs, some *Plate 124* have embroidered breast-plates and all wear variously shaped caps. The civil and military officials are followed by confronting pairs of animals, two pairs of lions, two of unicorn monsters, two of camels, two of elephants, two of *ky-lin* and two *Plates 123, 125* of horses. Some are in standing position and some rest on the ground.

The model for these sculptures, like those of Yung-lo's predecessor, is frankly T'ang, but in the human figures a heaviness has taken the place of the sense of movement which animates the earlier figures. The shape of the block of stone has asserted itself on the sculptors much in the same way as it did in the Han dynasty horses. This perhaps increases the impression of immobility suited for a tomb and emphasizes the dignity of the figures, but it runs counter to the general Chinese sculptural ideal of the expression of movement. The patterns on the robes of civil and military figures and on the saddle cloths of the horses are again T'ang inspired, but rich workmanship and careful finish have become the prime consideration. As a result they remain surface decoration. The inner spirit is lacking and their effect owes most to the grave and simple manner in which they are presented.

The animals are inflated T'ang figures, but in enlarging them, something of the life and energy which inspires the T'ang tomb figurines has been lost. The quest for naturalism in sculpture, which one saw in some of the Sung dynasty figures, has here reached an impasse beyond which the Chinese did not proceed. Monumental sculpture seems to have died in China from the early 15th century, and nothing more of significance was produced. The Chinese never seem to have found a substitute for religious inspiration. The figures of the tomb of Emperor Yung-lo are nobly conceived and, if they do not stand comparison with the great religious works of the past, the fault lies in the high standard of the art with which they must be compared.

Notes on the plates on page 227

NOTES ON THE PLATES TO
CHAPTER VIII

119 MYTHICAL ANIMAL in stone at the tomb of the first Ming Emperor, Hung-wu, near Nanking, *c.* 1400. See *p. 214.*

120 MYTHICAL ANIMAL in stone from the same tomb.

121 PAIR OF WARRIORS in stone from the same tomb.

122 STONE WARRIOR in a coat of mail on the Sacred Way leading to the tomb of the Emperor Yung-lo, near Peking, *c.* 1424–1430. See *pp. 216/217.*

123 HEAD OF A STONE HORSE on the Sacred Way to the same tomb.

124 STATUES OF CIVIL DIGNITARIES lining the Sacred Way to the same tomb.

125 ANIMALS OF STONE lining the same Sacred Way. Cf. the tomb of General Ho Ch'ü-ping (*plates 22, 25, 29*).

IX CHINESE ARCHITECTURE. PEKING AND THE FORBIDDEN CITY

THE DEATH of Emperor Yung-lo in 1425 on his way back from an expedition into Outer Mongolia marked the beginning of the decline of Ming authority. His son ruled for only ten months and the throne then passed to his grandson who became Emperor Hsüan-tê. His reign too was relatively short—only eleven years. Yung-lo's great-grandson Chêng-t'ung was only eight years old when he came to the throne and the real power passed into the hands of the Empress Dowager. As a child in the Forbidden City, Chêng-t'ung had been brought up by the women of the Inner Court and the eunuch guardians. As he grew older the eunuchs gained more and more influence over him until finally they succeeded in isolating him from all knowledge of true conditions in the country outside the imperial palace.

In times of good government an administrator could always bring a serious dissatisfaction or a blatant injustice to the attention of the Emperor. This was now no longer possible, and a servant who brought forward a grievance went in danger of losing his position and even his life without the remotest chance of the Emperor hearing about it. In 1450 the eunuchs prevailed on Chêng-t'ung to lead a disastrous campaign against a Mongol chieftain in which the Son of Heaven himself was taken prisoner. In the ensuing peace the Chinese formally signed away their right to interfere in Mongol affairs. Although the Emperor was finally returned to China, the campaign effectively ended the early Ming aspirations to wipe out the memory of the Mongols and to dominate them completely.

Under Emperor Chêng-tê (1505–1520) the power of the eunuchs reached its peak. These men of little education were often recruited from lowly families in distant parts of China. Many of them resented the well-educated scholar-administrator class and, naturally enough, they were often embittered by the disabilities which their emasculation placed on them. They were mainly interested in enriching themselves and they openly extended the extremely evil practice of selling offices to the highest bidder. Those who succeeded in buying an administrative post were then forced to extort the areas in their charge in order to recoup their investment. The resentment this aroused, especially in the south of China, was to have lasting effects.

Although the reigns of the Emperors Chia-ching (1520–1566) and Wan-li (1572 to 1620) were longer and less disturbed, China during this period was increasingly on the defensive from the tribes beyond the Great Wall. Another serious danger also began to threaten the country. The Japanese were becoming a menace through large-scale, highly organized raids on the rich Chinese coast. These raids, often led by high-born Japanese war-lords, developed into a profitable industry for the Japanese who even sacked large cities like Yangchou and Ningpo. They culminated in an exhausting, costly war against the Japanese in Korea. Only the death of Hideyoshi, the Japanese military dictator, seems to have saved the Chinese from defeat by Japan.

The fall of the Ming dynasty in 1644 and the rise to power of the Manchus provide the last act of the drama in which for nearly two thousand years the northern tribes played such a vital role. And the Great Wall was to feature in the history of China for the last time before modern armaments rendered it completely ineffective.

The Manchus were of Tungusic stock. As with the emergence of previous nomad invaders, an inspired leader, Nurhachu (c. 1559–1626), organized the independent elements of these tribes into a united nation conscious of its strength and destiny. He also brought under his banner many of the other Mongol tribes, turning their history of past military glory to his own purpose. They gained control of Korea and ruled a large area beyond the northern frontier of China from a capital at Mukden. They frequently raided north China but, until the mid-17th century, the Ming had prevented their gaining a permanent foothold in the Central Kingdom.

In the mid-17th century the enfeebled Ming suffered a serious revolt under a leader named Li Tzu-ch'êng. Famine and the heavy taxes imposed on the population to meet the twin demands of the eunuchs and the campaigns in the north drove him and his supporters to this extremity. The rebel leader was an able general and administrator and he succeeded in capturing Peking in 1644. The last Ming emperor hung himself from a tower which still exists.

Fitzgerald points out that 'It is improbable that the Manchus would have succeeded in conquering any large part of China if the Ming dynasty had not been destroyed by internal troubles, which, in turn, were largely a consequence of the remote situation of the capital'.* Had Peking not been so far in the north, far removed from the most densely populated and richest parts of the country, the Ming rulers might have been more conscious of the plight and feeling in the country at

C. P. Fitzgerald: op. cit.

229

large. Even to maintain the supply of this remote capital against the natural direction of communications was a heavy economic burden lying most heavily on the south.

Li Tzu-ch'êng was not destined for long to enjoy the control of the capital he had captured nor did he succeed, as he had hoped, in founding a new dynasty. At the time of his revolt and capture of Peking, a general named Wu San-kuei was defending part of the Great Wall on the northern frontier. Li Tzu-ch'êng had been responsible for the murder of Wu San-kuei's father and had seized one of the general's favourite concubines. Motivated by desire for revenge as much as by fears for his own safety, the general made common cause with the Manchus and allowed them to pass unchallenged and in force through the Great Wall which had hitherto held them at bay. Together they recaptured Peking. Wu San-kuei pursued his enemy to the west where Li and his dynasty passed from the scene. However, the Manchus had entered China to stay. It took them at least forty years to establish their undisputed control over the whole of China. The south always remained hostile and the Manchus, for their part, never trusted this highly populated, cultured and rich area which they suspected of harbouring loyalty to the Ming dynasty. Unsuited though it was, Peking remained the capital. The Manchus restored it and developed it into the city it now is.

In historical perspective, the Manchus were the most successful of all the northern invaders who over the centuries invaded China. Only the destructive Mongols ever controlled as much of the country as did the Manchus, and they did so for only a third of the time. Although the Manchus tried to keep themselves aloof from the native population, in fact, like the Northern Wei before them, they came to consider themselves as the true inheritors and preservers of Chinese culture. They became, indeed, more Chinese than the Chinese—supporters of the arts, champions of Confucianism, chroniclers of the past, ultra-conservatives. It must be said that, on the whole, they governed China ably and justly, and under their strict and sometimes reactionary rule the country found peace within which to prosper. Only the invasion by the powers of the West in the 19th century shattered their calm, complacent sense of inviolability.

Most of the architecture which has survived in China dates from the Ming and Manchu, or to give it its Chinese name, the Ch'ing, dynasties. However, as one might expect, excavations and literary records show that its history goes back to the beginnings of Chinese culture in the 2nd millennium BC. Unfortunately for the historian, wood has always been the principal material used for construction since these earliest times and the elements have been severe on it. Stone has been used much less than wood, but a few pagodas have survived in stone and brick since pre-T'ang times. An occasional wooden building has lasted from the T'ang centuries. Only from the Sung period onwards are the surviving wooden buildings sufficiently numerous for study purposes. The only fact which favours the historian is that the use almost exclusively of wood has encouraged traditionalism in building practice. Apart from the monuments now being discovered in little-explored parts of China, for the earliest evidence of wooden architecture in the T'ang dynasty, historians are forced to rely heavily on the temples built in Japan in strict emulation of Chinese models. Such buildings, constructed at a time when Japan was virtually a cultural colony of China, have survived in greater numbers and have been preserved more carefully than on the mainland. From the 14th century onwards a great deal remains—enough to give witness of an art which is worthy of greater attention than it has hitherto received.* Strangely enough the Chinese, among the world's most prolific writers on art, have over the centuries written very little about their own architecture. Hardly any of their architects are known by name and the whole art seems to have been relegated to the concern of the lowly craftsman. The fact that it has remained exclusively the concern of craftsmen has tended to emphasize the inherent traditionalism of design and technique.

> Among the few authorities who have treated Chinese architecture seriously are A. C. Soper in *The Art and Architecture of China*. London, 1956; O. Siren in *The Walls and Gates of Peking*, London, 1924; *The Imperial Palaces of Peking*, Paris and Brussels, 1926; and W. Willetts in *Chinese Art*, London 1958. To all three I am indebted for this brief account of a few features of Chinese architecture here reproduced.

Thus, by comparison with the West, architecture in China has shown a marked continuity of design and material. As Soper says, 'If traditionalism and resistance to change have been the prime characteristics of the Chinese way of life from beginning to end, there is no more vivid illustration of their working than that given by the history of architecture'.*

> A. C. Soper, op. cit., p. 205.

One of the first impressions a visitor gains of Chinese buildings *en masse* is that of their basically similar arrangement. The Chinese, as we know, have been dominated by the idea of seeking security behind walls. Just as the Great Wall limits the country in the north, so, as if in miniature, many towns have or had their walls of various sizes. The concept of a walled town is a familiar one to the West, but the Chinese take it one step further by walling also their dwelling units, and they do this in such a way that the walls often conceal what they enclose.

Cities themselves are generally laid out in regular squares, although growth, modifications and interruptions to the original layouts often obscure the regularity. Cities tend to extend laterally rather than vertically and multi-storied buildings are exceptional. The vault and arch have been known in China since early times but except for bridges and tombs they were seldom used and never exploited in the manner, for instance, of a Western cathedral. No compulsion ever seems to have urged the Chinese to build their buildings ever higher—even for emperors. Pagodas, of course, were multi-storied, but they are not intended for living purposes. The fear of earthquakes may have weighed heavily against tall buildings. Generally speaking, Chinese domestic and temple architecture is an art which has remained shut in on itself and except for pagodas has borrowed little from other countries and traditions.

For at least two thousand years Chinese cities and buildings have been laid out on a north–south axis. The principal buildings, such as imperial palaces, always face south. This has a symbolic meaning, for the palace on earth corresponds in Chinese thought to the Pole star in the heavens, and just as all the other stars seem to turn about it, so the buildings subordinate to the imperial palace lie to the south of it. Thus the emperor faces the south and the world he governs. The Chinese regarded the north to which he turned his back as the source of evil influences—as indeed the incursions of the barbaric peoples from that quarter had proved. The north–south axis dominates the whole city of Peking although this is apparent only from the air. On the ground the huge gates and the administrative complexes of palaces and Forbidden City break it up.

The homestead itself often resembles a city or an imperial precinct in miniature. It has its small courtyards and buildings all surrounded by a screening wall and the quarters of the head of the family are almost invariably on the main axis and often at the northern end of it. This tends to produce a somewhat monotonous effect, especially from the outside, but within the walls this is relieved by gardens in the smaller compounds and by parks in the larger imperial dwellings. A desire to bring the country into the city is one of the fundamental artistic impulses of both Chinese and Japanese domestic architecture, and it is one which adds great charm to the otherwise somewhat monotonous cities of the Far East. As if to offset the regularity of city and homestead, these gardens are designed with studied carelessness—a man-made effort of infinite patience to reproduce, even if only in miniature, the beautiful vagaries of nature.

One of the most characteristic and distinctive of all Far Eastern architectural forms is the pagoda, known in Chinese as t'a. Its origins are obscure and both Indian and Chinese elements have contributed to it. The more familiar wooden type with open pavilions rising one above the other in a diminishing sequence has a very long history in China and we see examples represented in bas-reliefs on stone and brick from the Han dynasty onwards when the form was popular for watch towers and pleasure pavilions in the parks which we know surrounded the imperial palaces of

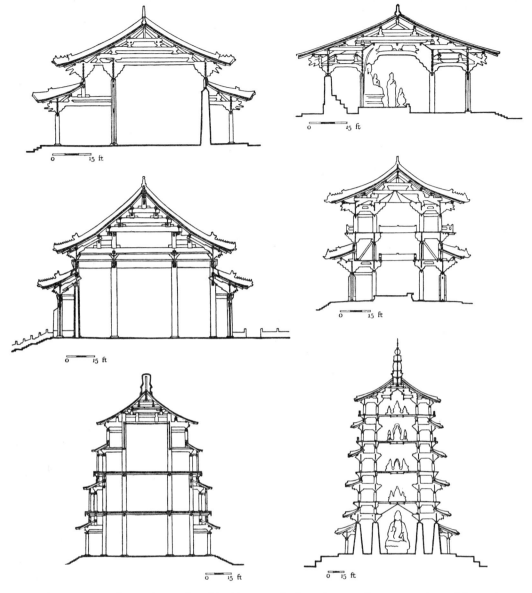

13 The structures of typical curved roof buildings. Left, from the top: the Great Palace of the Fo-kuang temple, Wu-t'ai-shan, Shansi province; tower of Kuan-yin, Tu-lo temple, I-hsien, Hopei province; Sākyamuni Pagoda, Fo-kung temple, Ying-hsien, Shansi province. Right, from the top: Shêng-mu Hall, Chin-tz'u, Tai-yüan-hsien, Shansi province; Lêng-ssu Palace, overlooking the Ming-ch'ang-ling and the Ch'ang-p'ing, Peking; Fo-hsiang Tower, I-ho-wan, Peking.

past ages. According to literary sources, tall hunting pavilions and towers existed even well before Han times. No early wooden pagodas have survived in China, but the famous five-storied pagoda of the Japanese Hōryū-ji temple has at least preserved faithfully the Chinese style of the 7th century.

The Indian stone structure known as the *stūpa* from the earliest Buddhist times was considered the most holy building of a temple precinct. This was basically a masonry dome on a square base large enough for worshippers to walk around in the performance of their religious services. The dome itself contained relics of the Buddha and was surmounted by a spire with mushroom-like projections along it. These represented umbrellas which indicated the royalty of the being whose remains it housed.

As Buddhism spread over Asia, the converts in the various areas which adopted the faith followed the injunctions of the holy texts to create similar stūpas. Very early in the history of Buddhism in China, the converts adopted the native wooden tower form to serve as stūpas, and the only feature distinguishing its Buddhist connotation was the spire with the miniature umbrellas, often multiplied to give added efficiency.

Plate 126

As with sculpture, at times when contacts with India were easy, the Chinese attempted to follow Indian techniques and designs more closely than in the native wooden tower form. The most famous example of this is the Ta-yen T'a, the 'Great Gander Pagoda', at Ch'ang-an. It owes its origin to the initiative of the most famous of all pilgrims, Hsüan-tsang, who wanted to build a stone stūpa in which to deposit the books and statues he had brought back from India. The Emperor supported his wish though he changed the material from stone to yellow brick, and when first finished in 652 it had only five storeys. Extensive restorations in 701 to 705 added another two storeys and gave the pagoda a total height of 190 feet. T'ang architects favoured wood as a building material and the influences of wood can be seen in the simulated pillars and capitals beneath the eaves of the various storeys. The whole construction is, of course, almost solid.

Such a type of tower construction is one of the oldest in the world and certainly goes back a long time before Buddhism in India. The towers of early West Asian civilizations must have been fundamentally similar. The Ta-yen T'a, as Soper says of another contemporary building, 'shows perfectly the early T'ang instinct to design in big, clear, simple forms'. Its sturdy proportions and bold lines illustrate the masculine taste of T'ang in which decoration is strictly disciplined by the desire to bring the various parts into a harmonious whole.

Plates 127, 128, 135, 136

A common tradition of beam and bracket construction links the early Han towers to the temples of the Ming and Ch'ing times. But the most immediately striking aspect of these and of almost all Chinese buildings is, of course, the gently curving roof, ending in wide eaves. All the examples reproduced here have this curve in lesser or greater degree. The reasons for and origins of this characteristic feature of Chinese building practice have been the subject of much speculation. The climate, with its bright sun and heavy rainfull, demands wide eaves, and it has been suggested that the eaves, shelter from rain, were made to turn upwards in order to let light into the buildings. Willetts has put forward the view that the curve is in fact the result of what was originally a sag in the roof created by using bamboo in long split lengths placed alternately concave and convex in such a way that they produce a roof which is a continuous series of gutters. The bamboo was light and, in order to secure it, weights were placed on the roof which created a sag. On the other hand Chinese writers attribute the curve to aesthetic considerations and link it with the typical curves of Chinese calligraphy for example. The earliest wooden buildings which we find represented on stone and bronze do not show curved roofs, and aesthetic considerations must have weighed heavily with the designers—especially when heavy tiles were the customary roofing material. Chinese roofs are not built on triangular roof trusses as are Western roofs but on a series of diminishing queen-posts and beams. These spread the thrust and carry the weight and provide a system in which the roof can be given any degree of curve. However, it is easier to build a roof with straight lines, and without doubt tiles, especially large ones, fit better on straight than on curved rafters. The only constructional advantage of a curved roof is that it enables the builders to use short lengths of timber, but there seems to have been no shortage of long timber in China until comparatively recent times.

It is axiomatic of building construction that structurally difficult features must be dictated by taste. An outstanding example of this is the intriguing doorways among which the completely circular form is only the most popular of many strange shapes. This difficult form, which has been tried in other countries with unfortunate results, seems to fit completely into the framework of curves and straight lines of Chinese buildings. The fantasy of such doorways or 'Moon Gates' produces a fairy-tale effect for the more practical Westerner for whom the view through a doorway is perhaps less important than its use fundamentally as a means of exit and entry.

Plates 130, 131

Beam and pillar construction gives the basic form to large wooden buildings. As a result, the exterior walls, protected from the weather by their deep overhanging eaves, can be light, non-structural, non-weight-bearing features. They can be, and often are, particularly in Japan, little more than screens which can be removed completely in the hot weather. Where walls surround the compounds, problems of security do not exist. Thus the traditional Chinese system antedates modern Western building practice of steel framework and walls which can be of any light material.

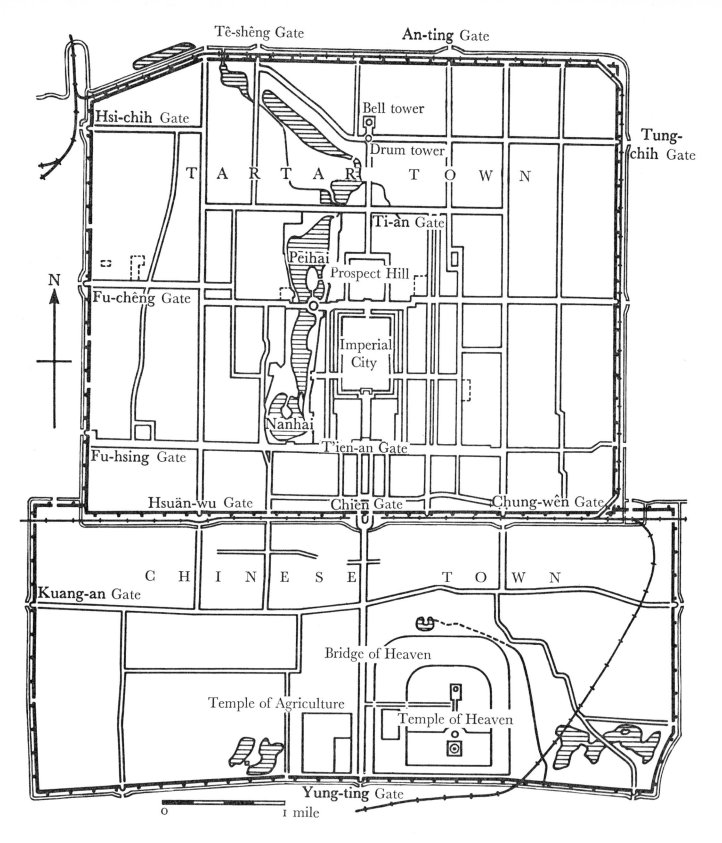

Tê-shêng Gate   **An-ting** Gate

Hsi-chih Gate

Bell tower

Drum tower

Tung-chih Gate

T A R T A R   T O W N

Ti-àn Gate

Peihai

Prospect Hill

N

Fu-chêng Gate

Imperial
City

Nanhai

Fu-hsing Gate

T'ien-an Gate

Hsuän-wu Gate   Chien Gate   Chung-wên Gate

C H I N E S E   T O W N

Kuang-an Gate

Bridge of Heaven

Temple of Agriculture

Temple of Heaven

Yung-ting Gate

0   1 mile

14   Plan of central Peking.

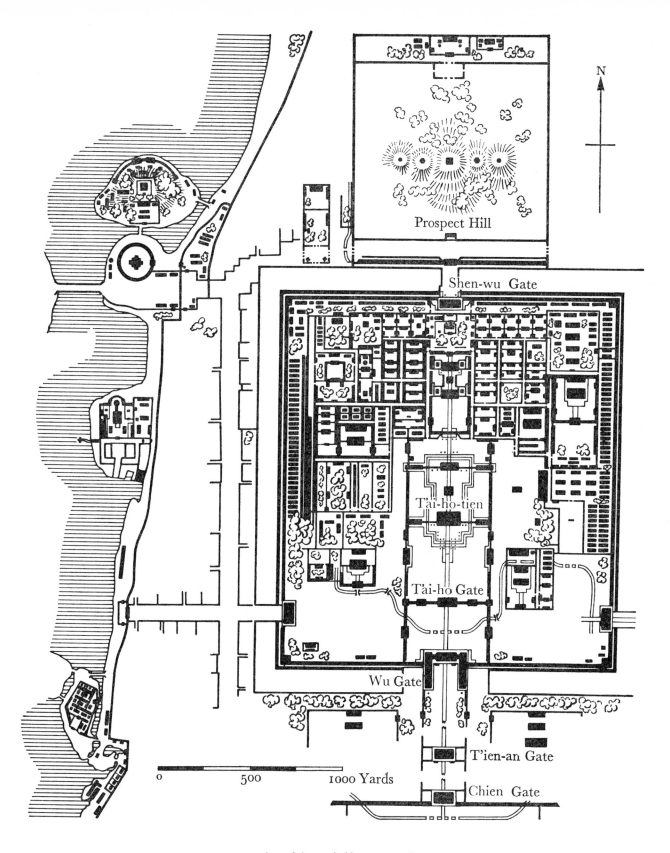

N

Prospect Hill

Shen-wu Gate

T'ai-ho-tien

T'ai-ho Gate

Wu Gate

T'ien-an Gate

Chien Gate

0   500   1000 Yards

15   *Plan of the Forbidden City, Peking.*

The huge pillars which are the main feature of temple halls support heavy beams which do not simply rest on them but are mortised and tenoned together. Where the hall is deep the need for added support requires pillars within the hall as well as on the outside. Thus *plate 129* shows a typical Chinese temple interior with a large central colonnade and smaller colonnades on either side. It shows the heavy transverse beams on which are built the series of smaller pillars and beams mounting in a pyramid to carry the heavy roof. This method of spreading the stress is somewhat similar to English medieval roof construction.

Architecturally speaking China is a relatively unexplored country. The present regime is expanding its research into and preservation of China's antiquities, especially in localities removed from the better-known centres. In time it should be possible to add much to our inadequate knowledge of Chinese architecture.

Peking itself has always fascinated the visitor, though its elusive charm seems to defy description. It is an old site going back to at least the 8th century BC when already it was the capital of a small northern state. The First Emperor in the 3rd century BC razed it to the ground, and it was rebuilt in the 1st century AD. It survived through the centuries occupied either by Chinese or by northerners depending on the strength of the Chinese in that area near the Great Wall. In about AD 1000 it was known as Yen-ching, 'The Swallow Capital'. From 1268 to 1272 Kublai Khan built his capital adjacent to and stretching north of the old city. This basically Mongol city formed the foundation of the present city although in its present condition it owes most to the building mania of the Ming emperors. Nevertheless it is interesting to recall here Marco Polo's impressions of the Mongol capital in which he served the Great Khan:

The Book of Ser Marco Polo. Ed. Col. Yule. London, 1871, p. 332. Quoted by Siren: *The Imperial Palaces of Pekin.* 1926, Vol. I, p. 1.

'The streets are so wide and straight that you can see right along them from one gate to another. And up and down the city there are beautiful palaces and many great and fine houses in great number. All the plots of ground on which the houses are built are four-square, and laid out in straight lines. . . . Each square plot is encompassed by handsome streets for traffic; and thus the whole city is arranged in squares just like a chessboard, and disposed in a manner so perfect and masterly, that it is impossible to give a description that would do it justice.'*

It may well be that he exaggerated, but the city has remained basically as he described it, and his literary followers down to the present day have had no greater success in giving an account of the city which captures its elusive atmosphere.

Plates 133, 135–139

The most impressive architectural complex in Peking, and perhaps in the whole of China, is that of the Forbidden City. The whole area is a huge quadrangle measuring three quarters of a mile from north to south and a half mile east to west sur-rounded by a high wall and a wide moat. It is situated almost in the very centre of the modern city of Peking breaking its north–south axis. Within its four walls are the Imperial precincts. Outside the area of the Forbidden City is a much larger walled quadrangle which encloses the Imperial City. The general layout as now seen is about seven hundred years old. Between the outer walls of the Imperial City and those of the Forbidden City are a number of lakes and hills, some of which form the pleasure park known as the Winter Palace. In *plate 138*, taken from within the Forbidden City and looking over its walls, one can see in the background the top of the White Dagoba built on one of these hills in 1652.

The main entrance to the Forbidden City is the Wu-mên, 'The Gate of the Zenith' or 'The Gate of the Midday Sun'. This southernmost gate is a two-storied building placed on a high, wide battlement through which are three gateways. Built in 1647 and rebuilt in 1801, the Wu-mên gives access to the precincts and from it one has the imposing view shown in colour on *plate 133*. Here the visitor starts his approach to the palace, crossing on a broad pavement a series of spacious empty courtyards decorated only by the white marble pillars and balustrades of the cause-ways, bridges, stairways, etc. The first and largest of these courtyards is crossed by a marble channel through which flows the 'River of Golden Water' which is spanned by five marble bridges. In former times official business was conducted in this courtyard.

At the far end of this courtyard the T'ai-ho Mên or 'Gate of Supreme Harmony' brings the visitor one stage nearer the imperial presence. In front of it is a stone box in which during former dynasties petitions could be placed for the attention of the emperor. This two-storeyed gateway approached by three stairways is less fortress-like than the main gate. The central staircase is made up of a ramp carved in bas-relief with narrow stairs on either side and up this the Emperor would have been carried. This building also is of Ming origin with restorations made during the last dynasty. From here on the courtyards become smaller. The next leads directly to the T'ai-ho Tien, 'The Hall of Supreme Harmony'. This two-storied building and the two succeeding buildings are placed on a higher pediment, surrounded by a forest of white marble balustrades, and this 'Dragon Pavement' is reached by another triple staircase. This is the first audience hall proper, built in 1627 and rebuilt four times since then. Its low, broad proportions give it a peculiar majesty, and here most solemn ceremonies were enacted on the Chinese New Year's Day, the winter sol-stice and the Emperor's birthday.

Beyond this and on the same high pediment is the Chung-ho Tien or 'Hall of Middle Harmony' a smaller square building also of Ming date but restored in 1627 and 1765. Here the emperor held a symbolical inspection of the agricultural implements and seeds for the coming year, prepared the messages to be read at the memorial services in the Ancestral Temple and prepared himself for the ceremonies to be held in the 'Hall of Supreme Harmony'. Beyond this is yet another hall, the third of the central group, the Pao-ho Tien or 'Hall of Protecting Harmony' which is also of Ming design but restored in the 18th century. Here the Emperor received vassal princes and those of his subjects who had gained the highest awards in the examinations for the civil service, the future administrators of the country.

Beyond these three buildings lie the living quarters of the Emperor and his women-folk—an area strictly forbidden to all, except members of the imperial family and their staff.

On first sight the similarity of many of the buildings and their marble stairways and balustrading causes confusion, but many authors have testified to the powerful emotional effect, the mounting tension this series of courtyards and buildings creates. *Plate 139* gives a view of the staircase leading from the east courtyard of the 'Three Great Halls'. The building on the right is the Pao-ho Tien and the central Chung-ho Tien is in the shadows at the top of the central stairs. The rich ornamentation of the marble pillars is clearly visible.

It is undoubtedly the cascades of gleaming white terraces with their rows of balustrades and richly carved newel heads stretching into the distance like a frozen plateau which holds together the whole Forbidden City. They are dominated by the red buildings whose tints are often toned down by sun and rain to brownish reds or greys and the whole crowned by yellow glazed tiles which glitter in the sunlight. The breadth and unity of concept, the scintillating colours and the restrained grandeur make this one of the world's most impressive architectural masterpieces.

The last architectural monument here reproduced forms part of the site of the Altar of Heaven, outside the Imperial City in the southern City of Peking. This site comprises first a large square, within which is a circle, followed by a series of diminishing circular terraces all in white marble. The top terrace is open and forms the Altar of Heaven proper. During the last dynasty this was the most important area, where the Emperor officiated at the solemn sacrifice to heaven on the longest night of the year. It contains the tablets to Shang-ti, 'The Supreme God', tablets to the imperial ancestors, the sun, moon and Five Planets, Ursa Major, the twenty-four constellations, the signs of the zodiac, the gods of the clouds, rain, and thunder. At other times of the year less important ceremonies were enacted on this broad round platform.

Proceeding north of this one reaches a round temple building with a single conical roof. This is followed by a large gate, a long road and finally another square enclosure with again a triple terrace on which stands a larger round hall with three conical roofs. The whole site, 4 miles in circumference, has the same white balustrading as the Forbidden City, but here the posts are set off by red surrounding walls and deep blue tiles on the roofs.

The central small round hall contained the Altar of Earth at which the emperor sacrificed on the summer solstice. The larger round hall is of Yung-lo period design but restored in the mid-18th century and again at the end of the 19th century. In Ming times it was used for the all important Sacrifice to Heaven, but in the mid-18th century its name was changed to the present Ch'i-nien Tien and its function was changed, being then dedicated to composite ceremonies to heaven and earth, the spirits, the spring and autumn crops and prayers for bountiful harvests. The interior is richly decorated with red lacquer and often with leaf and flower patterns in gold relief. The beams and brackets are in blue, green, white and gold on a red background. The muted light within the hall softens what might be a garish effect into a wealth of soft colour.

Plate 140

Despite its lateness the building has a resplendence which Soper has admirably described as a 'spectacular beauty, drawn from geometry and colour: dazzling white, red, and deep blue for the conical roofs that seem to dramatize the lustre of a night sky'.*

A. C. Soper, op. cit., p. 288.

We have now followed the development of some aspects of Chinese art through about two thousand years—from the massiveness of the Great Wall, through the transcendental dignity of early Buddhist sculpture, the exuberant vitality and delicate flow of its later manifestations, to the heavy grandeur of Ming and Ch'ing. At all times the Chinese spirit has expressed itself in breadth of scale, mastery of technique and above all in a power which is the product of confidence and restraint. These are the qualities which at all times have placed the stamp of individuality on the monumental art of China.

Notes on the plates on page 259

127

135

NOTES ON THE PLATES TO CHAPTER IX

APPENDIX

SOURCES OF CHINESE BUDDHIST ART

In the present state of our knowledge it is impossible to trace in any detail the spread of Buddhist art styles from India to China. Most of the links in the vast areas of Central Asia, which lay between them, no longer exist, and the dates of those that do are uncertain. Nor do we know enough about the chronology of the Buddhist art of Gandhāra in North India, especially the relationship between the early and late Gandhāran sculpture (see below), whence many of the influences on Chinese art must have derived. The danger is of over-simplifying a most complicated problem.

Plate 141

Plate 142

Plate 143

Plates 144, 145

The Indian origin of cave temples is clearly established at such sites as Ajanta, to mention only the best known of hundreds. The cave temples at Bāmiyān in Afghanistan certainly influenced strongly the Central Asian converts as did also the colossal figures of the Buddha which dominate these caves. The efforts which the faithful made to emulate them in such Central Asian sites as Kyzil and Khotan are notable in their own right but as far as we can now judge were not comparable in size and workmanship with their Indian models or with the caves of China. Nevertheless their influence on China must have been very great for many of the Chinese pilgrims never reached farther than these Buddhist outposts in the Central Asian wilderness.

Plates 146–148

Stylistically Chinese Buddhist art owes much to the Romano-Hellenistic art of Gandhāra in northwest India. The typical Gandhāra draped figures of the 2nd to 3rd centuries certainly provided the model for Khotan and thence for early Yün-kang.

Plate 156

Plates 149, 150

At the same time a truly Indian art, which developed to the south of Gandhāra at places like Mathurā, especially in its later form, exercised an influence on Gandhāran styles and vice versa. Thus a second type of Gandhāran art best known from its stucco sculpture at sites like Taxila and Fondūkistan became more Indian in character. This style was more widely dispersed than the early stone Gandhāra work and lasted longer. The stucco technique simplified the repetition which is a characteristic of Buddhist sculpture in Central Asia and also in China. In the hands of sensitive workmen stucco was capable of more elegant forms and a more spiritual expression than the earlier Gandhāra sculptural styles.

As communications between China and India improved the later Gandhāran style together with truly Indian Gupta styles (examples of which the pilgrims brought back with them) exercised an increasing influence on Chinese sculpture until by the T'ang dynasty (618–907) the Chinese sculptors were able to produce their own elegant synthesis.

Plate 151

Plates 152, 154

Within these centuries of Chinese Buddhist sculpture (4th–13th centuries) the style of the late Northern Wei as seen at Yün-kang and Lung-mên (*c.* 490–540) stands out as a beautiful phenomenon in which the native Chinese aesthetic for a brief spell seems to assert itself most strongly. In many ways the 6th century is the most original and the most 'Chinese' of all the centuries of Chinese sculpture.

Plates 153, 157

261

Notes on the plates on page 267

143

141

142

144

145

146

148

NOTES ON THE PLATES TO APPENDIX

BIBLIOGRAPHY

ANDREWS, F. H., *Wall Paintings from Ancient Shrines in Central Asia Recovered by Sir Aurel Stein*. London, 1948.

BACHHOFER, L., *A Short History of Chinese Art*, New York, 1946.

BALAZS, E., et al., *Aspects de la Chine*, 2 vols. Paris, 1959.

BASHAM, A. L., *The Wonder that was India*. London, 1954.

BOUILLARD, G., *Tombeaux Impériaux*. Peking, 1931.

CHANG SHU-HUNG, *Ton-ko no Heki-ga*. Tokyo, 1958.

CHAVANNES, E., *Mémoires historiques de Ssû-ma Ch'ien*, 5 vols. Paris, 1895–1905.

CHÊNG CHÊN-TO, *Mai-chi-shan Shih-ku*. Peking, 1934.

CONZE, E., *Buddhism, its Essence and Development*. Oxford, 1951.

COWELL, E. B., and ROUSE, W. H. D., *The Jataka*. Cambridge, 1901.

CRESSEY, G. B., *China's Geographical Foundation*. New York, 1934.

CULTURAL OBJECTS PRESS, *Chung-kuo Chien-chu*, Peking, 1958.

DAVIDSON, J. L., *The Lotus Sūtra in Chinese Art*. New Haven and Oxford, 1954.

FITZGERALD, C. P., *China—A Short Cultural History*. London, 1935.

FOUCHER, A., *L'Art gréco-bouddhique du Ghandhâra*. Paris, 1951.

GELL, W. E., *The Great Wall of China*. London, 1909.

GILES, H. A., *Travels of Fa Hsien*. Cambridge, 1923.

GOETZ, H., *India: Five Thousand Years of Indian Art*. London, 1959.

GRAY, B., and VINCENT, J. B., *Buddhist Cave Paintings at Tun-huang*. London, 1959.

GROUSSET, R., *Les Civilisations de l'Orient*, 4 vols. Paris, 1926.

L'Empire des Steppes. Paris, 1939.

Sur les Traces du Buddha. Paris, 1929.

La Chine et son Art. Paris, 1951.

HACKIN, J., *Studies in Chinese Art and Some Indian Influences*. London, 1937.

HERRMANN, A., *Historical and Commercial Atlas of China*. Harvard, 1935.

IKECHI, H., and UMEHARA, S., *T'ung-kou*, 2 vols. Tokyo and Hsin-ching, 1938.

JENYNS, S., *Selections from 300 Poems of the T'ang Dynasty*. London, 1946.

LATOURETTE, K. S., *The Chinese, Their History and Culture*. New York and London, 1934.

LATTIMORE, O., 'Origins of the Great Wall of China' in *The Geographical Review*, 1937.

LE COQ, A. VON, *Die buddhistische Spätantike in Mittelasien*, 7 vols. Berlin, 1922–1933.

McGOVERN, W. M., *The Early Empires of Central Asia*, U.S.A., 1939.

MIZUNO, S., *Bronze and Stone Sculpture of China*. Tokyo, 1960.

MIZUNO, S., and NAGAHIRO, T., *Unko Sekkutsu. Yün-kang*, 16 vols. Kyoto, from 1952.
A Study of the Buddhist Cave Temples at Lung-mên, Honan. Tokyo, 1941.

NEFF, M., 'The Origins of the Indian Cave Temple' in *Oriental Art*, vol. IV, I, 1958.

PAINE, R. T., and SOPER, A. C., *The Art and Architecture of Japan*. London, 1955.

PEI-P'ING-SHIH-CHÊNG-FU PI-SHU-CH'U, *Chiu-tu Wen-wu-lioh*. Peking, 1934.

PELLIOT, P., *Les Grottes de Touen Houang*, 6 vols. Paris, 1914–1924.

ROBINSON, R., *Chinese Buddhist Verse*. London, 1954.

ROWLAND, B., *The Art and Architecture of India*. London, 1935.
'Indian Images in Chinese Sculpture' in *Artibus Asiae*, vol. X, I, 1947.

RUDOLPH, R., *Han Tomb Art of West China*. Berkeley and Los Angeles, 1951.

SANSOM, G., *A Short Cultural History of Japan*, London, 1946.

SAUNDERS, E., and DALE, *Mudrā*. New York, 1960.

SICKMAN, S., and SOPER, A. C., *The Art and Architecture of China*. London, 1956.

SIREN, O., *Chinese Sculpture from the Fifth to Fourteenth Centuries*, London, 1925.
The Walls and Gates of Peking. London, 1924.
The Imperial Palaces of Peking. London, 1924.
Chinese Painting: Leading Masters and Principles, 7 vols. London, 1956–1958.

STEIN, A., *Serindia*. Oxford, 1921.
Ruins of Desert Cathay. London, 1912.

SWANN, P. S., *An Introduction to Japanese Art*. Oxford, 1958.

WALEY, A., *The Way and its Power*. London, 1934.
Three Ways of Thought in Ancient China. London, 1946.
Translations from the Chinese. New York, 1941.
A Catalogue of Paintings Recovered from Tun-huang by Sir A. Stein. London, 1931.

WATSON, W., *Sculpture of Japan*. London, 1959.

WILLETTS, W., *Chinese Art*. London, 1958.

ZIMMER, H., *The Art of Indian Asia* (2 vols.), completed and edited by JOSEPH CAMPBELL. New York, 1955.

ZÜRCHER, E., *The Buddhist Conquest of China*. Leyden, 1959.

INDEX